An Alien at St Wilfred's

WITHDRAWN

An Alien at St Wilfred's

Adrian Plass

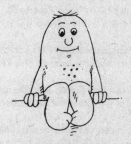

Illustrated by
Paul Judson

Fount
An Imprint of HarperCollinsPublishers

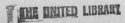

Fount Paperbacks is an imprint of
HarperCollins*Religious*
Part of HarperCollins*Publishers*
77–85 Fulham Palace Road,
Hammersmith, London W6 8JB

First published in Great Britain
in 1992 by Fount Paperbacks
1 3 5 7 9 10 8 6 4 2

A catalogue record for this book
is available from the British Library

ISBN 0 00 627619 9

Printed and bound in Great Britain by
HarperCollinsManufacturing Glasgow

Dedication

This book is dedicated to Geof Pryor, who died as it was being written. He brought a lot of light and hope into my life, and I shall miss him greatly. David Persimmon's account of what happened to Vincent Jenkins in hospital is actually a description of an experience that changed Geof's life a few months before he died. I know that he wanted to share it with others. It is a privilege to be able to help him do that.

Contents

Part One

Enter An Alien

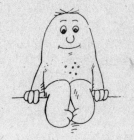

Enter An Alien

1

My name is David Persimmon. I am large, not very holy, and a clergyman in the Church of England. Nearly four years ago I became the vicar of St Wilfred's, Fernley-Cross, where I settled into a state of profound unhappiness almost immediately.

There were a couple of reasons for this, one of the main ones being my temperament. I tend to swing from bad temper to flabby acquiescence, with a stage of defensive facetiousness in between. My mother, bless her soul, said that I had a passionate nature. My father, curse his braces, said I was manic. I don't know which of them was right, but I do know that I find it very easy to put people's backs up, especially when I'm feeling threatened and incompetent, which brings me to the second reason for my early misery at St Wilfred's.

The organist.

People who've never done any vicaring find it difficult to believe that one person can cast a blight over the whole of one's ministry (if I can use such a word to describe my stumbling attempts to lead the people of this parish), but I can assure you that it happens. It happened to me. Nigel Forsyth happened to me. He'd been in the parish for about three hundred and ninety-five years before I arrived, and he had a firm grip on most aspects of church life. He wasted no time in establishing a firm grip on *me*. I started all wrong, of course. Meeting him for the first time at a welcoming party arranged by the resident dungeon-master, I decided to project my 'witty on the surface but clearly having great depth' image in order to impress this small, thin man with the stern eyes who had FANATICAL MODERATE written all over him.

'I don't know what your last vicar was like,' I said, 'but I always feel I let the old religious side down a bit.'

He raised an eyebrow humourlessly. 'Really?'

'Well, for instance,' I ploughed on foolishly, 'I read *Private Eye* and *Renewal*. I hide *Renewal* in *Private Eye*, and *Private Eye* in *Renewal*, depending on who I'm with at the time. If I've got the *Daily Mail* I just hide it.'

Cue laughter. It was one of my best spontaneous lines.

'I read the *Daily Mail* myself,' said Forsyth without even the ghost of a smile, 'and I certainly hope you don't intend to recommend *Private Eye* to the folk at St Wilfred's. We would consider it quite unsuitable. Incidentally, may I ask if you have a musical background, Reverend Persimmon?'

Demolished inwardly by what I am now sure was a quite deliberate bludgeoning of my feeble little joke, I responded with a quite startling lack of wisdom. In fact, I compressed as much neat malice as I possibly could into the casualness of my reply.

'No, but I've never really thought music should be that high a priority in the life of the church, have you?'

I then rounded off this presentation of myself as a complete idiot by allowing a sudden wave of guilt and worry to throw up the following memorable words.

'Only joking . . .'

Queen Victoria and Nigel Forsyth would have got on very well together. His expression of acid disapproval intensified, and I suddenly remembered overhearing the mother of a boyhood friend whispering to her son in the kitchen, 'He's very *big*, darling. Are you sure he's the same age as you?'

'Well, Reverend Persimmon,' said Forsyth, 'I sincerely hope that you are joking. We are extremely proud of our musical tradition here at St Wilfred's, and few, if any, of my fellow church members would welcome any dilution of that tradition. An immense amount of work has been done on building up and sustaining a level of choral expertise that is a fully professional one. The "life of the church", as you described it just now when you were joking, has been largely fuelled by musical input for some years, and I must say, it seems to me highly unlikely – and undesirable – that a change of direction would . . .'

On and on and on he went, his voice buzzing resonantly like some self-satisfied, moderate bee who refuses to extract nectar from any but classical blooms. He touched on the stability of the church, and the role of the church, and the fabric of the church, and the atmosphere of the church. He knew all there was to know about every aspect of all of these things.

Beyond fantasizing about confining him in a small locked room with 'The Sex Pistols' Greatest Hits' at full volume, there wasn't a great deal I could do. My confidence had snapped like something or other that snaps easily, as soon as I withdrew so pathetically from my 'joke'. Now, all I could do was squeak out agreement with every objectionable thing that he said.

'Yes, of course . . . well, absolutely, yes . . . naturally . . . I see exactly what you mean . . . I never thought of it like that . . .'

Miserably, I realized that, even at this early stage, the pattern of our relationship was set solid. He would say things, I would agree with him, then I would do things that went right against the 'agreement' that we'd made, and he'd be furious and scathing. I was right. That's exactly how it was. And, as a result, an awful lot of cats got kicked – innocent ones, usually. Being single, I wasn't able to deposit any of my unhappiness and frustration in the lap of a loved one (which was probably just as well for the hypothetical loved one), so I began to acquire a reputation in the parish – among some people, anyway – for being a weak man with a very bad temper. The phantom of Forsyth affected everything.

'If I say read it from the steps, I *mean* read it from the steps! If I'd meant read it from the lectern, I'd have *said* read it from the blasted lectern, wouldn't I? It's got absolutely nothing to do with what anybody else wants, unless another vicar has been appointed during my day off!'

Thus, I brutally harangued Margaret Vinny, who, when asked by me to read the lesson from the altar steps for a change, had responded uneasily with the words: 'Have you checked that it's all right with Nigel?'

When Sunday arrived, poor Margaret, nervous but obedient, duly read the first lesson from the top of the steps. Later, during the after-service coffee time, Forsyth approached me, tight-lipped and grim.

'I've just asked Margaret why she read the lesson from the wrong place,' he said, 'and she tells me you told her to. Is that true?'

I twitteringly confessed to this foul crime, and didn't have the courage to defend myself. Five minutes later, an inoffensive parishioner who was doing the coffees playfully asked me why I hadn't put ten pence in the dish like everyone else, and received a vitriolic and quite unwarranted blast of anger in return. It was dreadful!

I hated my first three years at St Wilfred's. I felt far away from God, and fell into the habit of not praying, which was and is absolutely disastrous for me. My sermons were a weekly nightmare. Standing in the pulpit each Sunday was like sitting in a car with no petrol in the tank, making 'brrmm-brrmm' noises. On my days off I shook the dust of Fernely-Cross from the soles of my size twelves, and spent as long as possible in that wonderful place called 'Elsewhere'. There were bright spots, of course, but, generally speaking, it was one of the grottiest periods in my life, and I associated it all with Nigel Forsyth – blamed him for it, if I'm honest. And that attitude stayed unchanged until – well, read on . . .

2

At eight o'clock on the evening of Thursday, November the first last year, I crossed the graveyard and went into the church for an hour or so of locked-in misery. It was as I switched on the aisle lights that I saw him. He was sitting on top of the steps, just where Margaret Vinny had committed her sin of misplaced oratory.

I stood without moving for a moment, my hand still on the lightswitch, and said just two words.

'An alien . . .'

He certainly *was* an alien in the sense that he was not a human being, but he didn't have nine legs and a television aerial sticking out of his head. He was shaped like a normal person, but he wasn't as large as an adult. He was unclothed, and yet needed no clothing. He was snowy white in colour, a completely uniform shade all over, and quite unblemished as far as I could see. As I walked slowly and nervously up the aisle towards him he stood, giving me a much clearer view. He was too teddy-bear-like to be described as childlike, but too near to the form of a young human being to be compared to some sort of cuddly toy. The most extraordinary thing about him was a warm, glowing light that seemed to emanate from *inside* his body. It must have started after I switched on the light, because he certainly hadn't been shining in the dark when I first came into the church.

I think I was too battered in spirit to get terribly alarmed by this extraordinary encounter, but, in addition, when I finally stood eyeball to eyeball with my strange visitor, I saw in his large, luminous eyes that he was a very nervous little alien indeed. We looked at each other for quite a long time without any verbal communication at all. Then he spoke in perfect English, his voice quiet and unhappy in tone, but marvellously clear.

'Please say some comfortable words.'

'Hello, my name is David.'

This inspired greeting produced another lengthy silence. Then my pale friend held his arms out as though he wanted to embrace me, and said, 'I have no name in your words, but that will not cause unhappy divisions between us. All this day I have learned your speech from many books.' He pointed over my shoulder to the library space at the back of the church. 'I have inwardly digested your prayer book, and your holy writings, and your

Diamonds Are For Ever, and your *Biggles Flies West*, and your *Psychological Constructs of Christian Belief* and some others. I would like to borrow a name from your prayer book, if you will allow it?'

I nodded rather dazedly. 'Help yourself . . .'

'May I be known as Nunc?'

'Nunc as in "Nunc Dimittus"?'

'Yes, please, David.'

'It's a pleasure – Nunc. Err . . . where have you come from?'

'I may not say.'

'How did you get into the church when it was locked?'

'It was the *right* place.'

'The right place?'

'Yes.'

'How did you get here from – from wherever you started?'

'I may not say.'

'But you do have some sort of . . . well, home, do you?'

The luminous eyes shone with tears suddenly.

'You're very unhappy, Nunc', I said, genuinely distressed by the sadness of his expression.

'So are you, David,' he replied, so unexpectedly that I took an involuntary, twitchy little step forward, and found myself wrapping my arms around the small figure who faced me. That physical contact was one of the warmest, most real things that had happened to me for a very long time. Sitting next to my odd new friend on the altar steps a minute later I felt unusually peaceful – if very confused and puzzled.

'Nunc,' I said, 'if you can't tell me how you got here or where you've come from, at least tell me *why* you're here.

You said this is the *right* place – what does that mean?'

Nunc answered seriously, 'I may not depart in peace until I have waited with four or five. I may not leave this building. I may not be seen or heard by any but those with whom I wait. I do not know when I shall go . . .'

Later that night I studied my face in the bathroom mirror at home. No less ugly than usual, but relatively sane looking. I'd just spent more than an hour talking to an alien – or had the pressure got to me at last? Tomorrow morning I would find out. Nunc had asked me to select three people to make up the group of those 'with whom he would wait', whatever that might mean, so that we could meet regularly in the church. When I asked what sort of people he had in mind, he just smiled and said, 'Friends, aliens, whoever you wish, David.'

Tomorrow I would bring my first 'selection' into the church and check out my own sanity.

3

Hartley Sutton lived in a small, family-type hostel not far from the vicarage, and was the most sweet-natured man I'd ever met. I don't know much about these things, but, according to Mrs Bletchley, who ran the hostel, he would have been quite incapable of living independently. This puzzled me for a long time, because Hartley sometimes displayed impressive verbal skills, and he had a truly amazing memory. Apparently this didn't necessarily signify, though. In his case there was a big gap between the saying and the doing, which made him incapable of anything but the simplest kinds of work. During the day he performed the most excruciatingly tedious tasks up at the council-run work centre, but he didn't seem to mind at all. In the evenings he often came over to the church to clean and dust for me. Hartley loved pottering about among the pews and the books, and he was very conscientious. I think he would be astonished if he knew how much his simple, natural kindness and humility meant to me during those three bleak years. I needed him much more than he needed me.

I took Hartley to St Wilfred's at seven o'clock on the Friday evening. I had decided to stay out of the church until I had someone with me. As we entered the porch I said, 'Hartley, old son, there's an alien called Nunc in our church. Either that – or I'm completely bonkers. If you see him too, then I'll know that he really exists, or else that we're *both* completely bonkers. That's quite likely.'

There was no need to switch the light on this time. Nunc was glowing like a snowman in the moonlight, as he stood at the far end of the church with his hands resting on the altar. We walked quietly up the aisle and sat on the front pew waiting for him.

'You *can* see him, can't you, Hartley?', I whispered.

'Yes, Reverend Persimmon,' hissed Hartley, 'I do not believe that we are both completely bonkers. I believe that he really exists. I am looking forward to meeting him.'

As the soft white light faded, Hartley scuttled back down the aisle to switch on the main lights, and by the time he returned Nunc was standing at the bottom of the steps waiting for him. You never saw two people beam at each other like those two did when they first met. They could have been two brothers meeting after a long separation, so pleased did they seem to encounter each other.

'My name is Hartley,' said Hartley at last, still in mid-beam, 'I am very pleased and honoured to make your acquaintance. You are the very first alien that I have known. Will you be living inside St Wilfred's?'

'Greetings, Hartley,' replied Nunc, 'I shall indeed be waiting here for a period. Shall we be friends?'

'I come in here some evenings,' explained Hartley, 'to clean and tidy for Reverend Persimmon.' He blushed slightly. 'I have been given my own key by the vicar, so I am able to come in when I wish, as long as Mrs Bletchley knows where I am. It will be nice to have a new friend. I already like you, Nunc.'

It was the beginning of something very special for Hartley. During the short time that our visitor was with us the two of them spent many hours together. Nunc offered Hartley a respect that was not even remotely patronizing, and as for Hartley's feelings about Nunc, well, he absolutely adored him – as you will discover.

4

The selection of my other two candidates for close encounters of the Nunc kind was very easy; Richard Craven and Dot Jenkins sprang to mind immediately.

Dick Craven was the only person in the parish who I'd ever been able to relax with. I first noticed him when he called out ludicrous answers to some of the inane questions I was addressing to the kids in a family service. I cornered him at the church door afterwards and found out that we had several things in common. We were about the same age, both single, we had the same rather anarchic sense of humour, and later I discovered that we both enjoyed eating long, lingering meals accompanied by good claret in restaurants where nobody knew who we were.

My contacts with Richard were always stimulating and enjoyable. He was a writer of science fiction (not one of my favourite branches of literature) with a head full of ideas and word-games. His depressed scepticism and my manic unhappiness produced sparks when they touched. Most of those lingering dinners were full of laughter and fascination as we explored the outer limits of some joke or idea or hypothetical situation. I suppose I kidded myself that we really knew each other, but it wasn't until Nunc came that I realized how hard Craven and I had worked to avoid touching the tender, hurt areas in each other. We were like two cowards with toothache distracting each other from contacting the dentist.

I phoned Dick later that same Friday evening on which Hartley and Nunc had met for the first time.

'Craven,' I said, 'there's an alien squatting in St Wilfred's. He's white all over, he's called Nunc, he's able to make his body shine, and he wants me to get a few people together to meet in the church every week. Fancy coming over to meet him?'

'I'd love to come,' replied Dick, 'but I have to deliver an African elephant to my aunt in Maidenhead. She gets very low unless she eats at least three every week, and I don't want to offend her because I'm hoping she'll leave me her collection of C. S. Lewis's notes to the milkman, so if you don't mind – '

'Dick, come over to the church. I want to show you something.'

'An alien who can make his body shine?'

'No,' I lied, 'just something I want you to see. Coming?'

Ten minutes later Dick, Nunc and I sat round one of the little square tables in the church hall, and I had the satisfaction of seeing Mr Cool Craven completely non-plussed. It only lasted for a little while, though. As Dick wrote later, there was a feeling of ordinariness – rightness – about Nunc. You tried to go on feeling amazed and flabbergasted by the presence of such a phenomenon, but you couldn't. Nunc was Nunc, warm and engaging, wise but vulnerable, enigmatic, yet as familiar and well-integrated as any ordinary person. Dick was slightly more wary at first than Hartley had been, but as Nunc's presence began to affect and change our lives he became as fond of him as the rest of us.

5

My final selection, Dorothy Jenkins, or 'Dot', as she was known to her friends, didn't meet Nunc until the Sunday evening following his arrival.

Dot was more than eighty years old, a committed and regular attender at St Wilfred's, although she'd kill me if I didn't point out that she had always been a Christian first and an Anglican second. She was one of those happy elderly people who bring a lot of joy into other people's lives. I got to know her when her husband, Vincent, developed cancer, not long after I came to the parish. Vince and I got on very well for some reason, and I spent a lot of time with him during the weeks leading up to his death. I suppose she had a bit of a soft spot for me after that, and the knowledge that someone appreciated me was like having a pair of water-wings. I just about stayed afloat.

It also meant that Dot was the only person I could easily take criticism from. Old and arthritic she might be, but when she had something say she said it without hesitation. She was not impressed by my sermons, my services, or my lack of courage on occasions, and she didn't mind telling me so. I didn't mind hearing what she had to say because I knew that, fundamentally, she valued me and thought I was capable of much more.

I whispered in Dot's ear as she shook my hand after the evening service on Sunday. 'Can you hang about for a bit, Dot? There's someone I'd like you to meet.'

We found Nunc sitting in the vestry with Hartley, learning to play dominoes.

'Dot,' I said, as I ushered her through the door, 'I'd like you to meet Nunc. Nunc, meet Dot, my favourite lady.'

Breeding will out, they say, and it certainly did in Dot. With hardly a blink she held out her white-gloved hand towards the small white figure who rose to greet her.

'I beseech you not to be fearful, Dot,' said Nunc quietly. 'I know that I am strange and an alien, but I am in great need of friends and friendship.'

Dot turned her head to look at me for a moment, her eyeballs seeming to revolve slightly as she mentally accommodated this unique experience, then she looked at Nunc again and her natural compassion and kindness asserted themselves.

'Any friend of Hartley's or David's,' she announced stoutly, 'is certainly a friend of mine.' She took his hand

and shook it warmly. 'Did you come in err . . . a spaceship?'

'I do not know,' said Nunc earnestly, 'but I do not think so. This became the right place to be, and therefore, I am here.'

Dot nodded, as though she found this information much less puzzling than I had, and then she pulled up a chair and assisted Hartley with his domino seminar. She really is a most remarkable woman.

6

Still in a total fog about what was going on, I agreed with the others that we would meet in the church every Thursday evening for as long as Nunc was with us, or until something happened to change things. Home-groups had dribbled to a standstill during my first year at St Wilfred's, so there was no question of poaching from other groups. Dot was very keen on the whole idea, so was Hartley. Dick Craven was the only one who expressed any doubts. He wasn't interested in either organized tedium, or emotional puking sessions – that was his elegant way of expressing reservations. I told him I wasn't very interested in those things either, and I threatened to make him pay for our next two evening jaunts if he caused any trouble. I knew he wouldn't be able to stay away, in any case – he was far too fascinated by Nunc to miss the experience.

The next couple of weeks would have supplied enough material for a book in themselves. 'Getting to know Nunc' provided us with a great deal of amusement, interest and not a few surprises. He never said very much, but every time he did speak, it was as though something important or significant had happened. Slowly, his language became more natural, although there was a strong prayer book flavour about it right up to the day he left.

The first two Thursday evening sessions were more social occasions than anything else. Craven held forth at great length to Nunc with his views on just about everything under the sun, I offered my modest opinion on a number of issues, and Dot alternated between telling us off for being flippant or silly, and helping Nunc to understand obscure words and phrases that were being used. Hartley just loved being there, and chipped in from time to time with a question or comment. They were very *warm* times.

Nunc was quite right when he said that no one else would be able to see him, although, with one exception, the question never arose because, as far as I know, nobody ever walked in on any meeting that we had with him. The exception was Sunday services and midweek meetings in the church. As I operated from the front I would see Nunc sitting on top of a bookcase at the far end of the church. He was there every time, looking like the ghost of some departed parishioner, and clearly quite invisible to the rest of the congregation. I liked him being there – I think.

It was the following four Thursday evenings that saw the strangest and most life-changing events in the course of our relationship with Nunc, and the story of those four evenings is recorded in the pages you are about to read. Hartley, Dot, Richard Craven and I have done our best to remember every detail of what happened. The other three have done a great job, even if my own contribution

suggests that I'm a sandwich or two short of a picnic!

Since the time when these accounts were written I do feel much more peaceful. I think Nunc helped a lot with that, but most of all I thank God, and pray it will last . . .

Part Two

Hartley's Account

Hartley's Account

1

Reverend Persimmon has asked me to write about the evening when he cried.

I remember the meeting on that Thursday very well indeed.

Before setting off for work that day I had a very important discussion with Mrs Bletchley in the kitchen. She is the nearest thing to a real mother that I have ever known, but I was a little worried about her reaction to the request I had in mind.

'Mrs Bletchley,' I said, 'may I just say that the breakfast you cooked for us this morning was quite wonderful.'

'Well, thank you, Hartley,' she replied, 'I'm glad you enjoyed it.'

She went back to the washing up, but I cleared my throat and she stopped again.

'Was there something else, love?'

'If I may say a word or two about the sausages . . . ?'

She dried her hands on her apron, sat down on the tall stool in the corner by the washing machine and listened with her whole face. No one else has done that in the homes I have been in, and no one else has managed to stop the others calling me Jam-pot, or Jammy, or Traffic-jam when we are out in the van. Mrs Bletchley says names are like pictures on the walls of houses where we are guests – we are not called upon to comment. She is the best staff I have known.

'The sausages were, if I may say so, the finest I have ever eaten, and –'

'Well, they were the same as we had last week, dear, from the Eight 'till Late shop in the High Street.'

'Ah!' I nodded seriously, 'that explains it.'

'Explains what, love?'

'Last week's were the finest I have ever eaten as well. As for the fried tomatoes – oh, Mrs Bletchley, you are like someone who cooks for a posh restaurant in London! And the coffee was – well, it was like rice.'

'I think you mean ambrosia, dear.'

'Ambrosia – yes, exactly – and you, Mrs Bletchley, are the one who prepared this feast?'

'Well, I got the breakfast, yes, Hartley. Err . . . did you want to ask me something, lovey?'

It was as though she had read my mind.

'Yes, Mrs Bletchley, it is about tea.'

'Tea?'

'Tea is at six-thirty, is it not?'

'Same as usual, yes, dear.'

I decided to be brave.

'Mrs Bletchley, I fear that if I have tea at six-thirty this evening I shall become institutionalized.'

Mrs Bletchley stared at me without speaking for a few seconds, and I noticed that her mouth was twitching in a strange way at the corners.

'Well, we can't have you getting institutionalized, now can we? What does that word mean by the way, Hartley? You and your books – I never know what you're going to come up with next.'

'It means,' I replied, 'an illness that you catch in homes if you have tea at the same time each day.'

She nodded.

'I see. And what time would you need to have tea this evening to avoid err . . . catching it?'

'Six o'clock would be perfectly safe,' I said firmly. 'I don't think I shall become institutionalized if I have my tea at six.'

She stood up, moved closer to me and took one of my hands in both of hers.

'Hartley,' she said, in a kind voice, 'what did they used

to say at your last place when you wanted to do something like having tea at a different time?'

I always want to break a plate when I think of my last place, and I cannot speak loudly when I am upset.

'He said,' I whispered, 'that meal times can't be changed, even for cross-eyed freaks with verbal over-flow problems and elephant-size memories.'

'He?'

'Mr Mountford. He was in charge of Gorton House.'

'Well, I don't care what Mr Mountford said. I think you're lovely, and if you've got a good reason for having your meals a bit earlier or later sometimes, then that's all right with me. Are you wanting to go along to your church meeting a bit earlier tonight?'

How does she know these things?

'Yes,' I said, 'I need to speak to my friend, Nunc.'

'Nunc?'

'An alien of my acquaintance, Mrs Bletchley.'

'Oh, I see, dear. Okay, tea at six o'clock then. No trouble, Hartley, no trouble at all. You'd better get off to work now, and I'd better get going on tonight's feast. Oh, and Hartley . . .'

I stopped in the doorway and turned round.

'Yes, Mrs Bletchley, may I serve you in some small way?'

'No, love, I just wanted to say that I *like* the way you talk. Just like a book. It's lovely!'

She is indeed a wonderful person.

My day at the work centre passed quietly, except for a rather silly incident at lunchtime when somebody (one of the childish ones, I think) smelled burning, and we all rushed around in different directions looking for the fire. I rushed around too until Grant Summers suddenly shouted: 'The smell's going wherever Hartley goes – Hartley's on fire!' and I realized that my pipe had set fire to the inside of my pocket. Ignoring the squeals of the others and remembering a great deal of first aid training, I picked up a nearly full bottle of milk from the kitchen hatch and emptied it into my pocket.

When Mrs Moon, our supervisor, came hurrying in from the office, Grant Summers was singing: 'Hartley's burning, Hartley's burning . . .' to the tune of some children's song, and I was dripping milk all over the floor. On learning what had happened Mrs Moon made the excellent suggestion that I should remove my jacket, and all ended well except that my pocket is not what it was.

2

Later, after my early tea, I crossed the big car park next to Turley's garage, where our van goes to be done, and climbed over the little brick wall behind the church. It was already dark by then, but I am not afraid of the dark. I am only afraid of no one caring about me in the dark – or the light, or anywhere really.

I was certainly not afraid of Nunc, because he spoke quietly and was kind, and sometimes he seemed to know nothing and at other times he seemed to know everything, and he made me laugh. I wanted to see him specially that evening about a small problem.

As usual I used my own personal key to get in through the little door at the back of the church, and as soon as I stepped inside I knew that Nunc was praying. He is the only friend I have ever had who glows like a night-light when he talks to God. As I tiptoed into the church I wondered if I should leave again. He was kneeling at the bottom of the altar steps shining like the glow-worm that my friend George's little girl has in bed with her, except that hers is worked by batteries and Nunc said he was connected to the mains, though he smiled when he said that and I never saw any wires or plugs.

I nearly crept out again, but Nunc must have heard me, because he looked over his shoulder, and the light faded from inside him like it did in the sitting room of my last home but one, when people played with the dimmer-switch even though they knew they would be severely punished if Auntie Marilyn caught them. I don't think Nunc was annoyed about me interrupting him though, because he smiled his big happy child smile and clapped his hands.

'Lighten our darkness, I beseech you, Hartley my friend,' he called. 'I render thanks for the great benefits I have received at your hands, but I am less sure about your feet, especially with the lights off. Why are you so wonderfully early?'

I carefully switched on the lights directly above the steps where Nunc was now sitting, and walked up the aisle to join him. Nunc was quite small, so I sat two steps below him.

'I am early,' I said, 'because I wished to have a private conversation with you before the others arrive.'

'I, for my part, am ready to listen,' said Nunc, tilting his head on one side and opening his eyes so wide that he suddenly looked exactly like Georgie the Ghost in a book I used to have. 'Proceed!'

'You are an alien,' I began.

'I am an alien,' he agreed.

'Not like us,' I added, in case he had not understood.

'Indeed not,' sighed Nunc. 'I have diligently examined myself and find that I have only one heart.'

'I think I only have one heart, Nunc,' I whispered. 'I saw it in a book.'

'But it says on page fifty-one of The Book of Common Prayer, in the second collect of Evening Prayer, that both our hearts must be set to obey the commandments of God, and I am quite sure that I have only one.'

Silently we pondered this mystery together.

'Well,' I said after a while, 'perhaps I am an alien as well, do you think?'

'If so,' he replied with another happy amile, 'we are a goodly fellowship, my friend. What is your question?'

'I wondered if – where you come from – it is important to be important, or . . . not.'

'Do you want to be important, Hartley?'

'I suppose I do, but – ' I lost my breath for a moment with the effort of being truthful – 'more than anything I do not wish to be an extra person who people in the church put up with.'

'We shall see,' said Nunc, lighting up inside slightly as he stood up and moved across to sit on the front pew opposite me.

'Tell me, who is the most powerful and important person in this Church of England of yours?'

That was easy.

'Reverend Persimmon says it is the organist, Mr Forsyth. He made me feel silly once when he told everyone that Hartley was a good name for me because the

Bible says that the Lord preserveth the simple, and he could probably make a few pounds of seedless out of me. Mr Persimmon did not laugh, but some people did. I became most hot and could only whisper.'

'And he is the most powerful member of this congregation of faithful men in which the pure word of God is preached?' asked Nunc wonderingly.

'Oh, yes! Reverend Persimmon came in very cross one day when I was tidying the magazine rack, and said that Forsyth and his choir made the Mafia look like a girls' friendly society, and he'd like to garotte the organist in mid-voluntary – in love. Then he said he shouldn't have said all that, and he was going home to repent because the only thing he was really sure about was that he was a sinner. Then he went out looking like an old coat. I think he was very sad.'

Nunc murmured something that sounded like, 'Hold not thy peace at my tears.' Then he said, 'And who is next?'

I thought carefully for a few moments.

'Several ladies, I think.'

Nunc said nothing.

'And then there are some people called churchwardens who make people take communion . . .'

'And then?'

'Several men, I think – in suits . . . and then I suppose it's Reverend Persimmon, and last of all the people who come to church.'

'And you? Where do you come, Hartley?'

'Bottom, Nunc – last of all. As you know, Reverend Persimmon has kindly given me a key of my own so that I can clean and tidy and just be here. I feel safe in the church, you see. And he says that he likes me being here, although I think he is just being kind . . . but really, yes, I come last. I have no important job to do.'

Nunc's eyes were like the glass in the ends of two telescopes.

'My dear Hartley,' he cried, 'I am unfeignedly thankful and proud to be your friend. The words in your own holy writings reveal the truth, "The first shall be last and the last shall be first . . . he hath exalted the humble and meek".'

Nunc suddenly bounced to his feet, walked forwards and knelt in front of me.

'Hartley,' he said, and I must say that he sounded extremely serious, 'you are the most important person in the Church of England!'

'Are you quite sure about this?' I asked. It was certainly the first I had heard of it.

'Oh, yes,' nodded Nunc. He stood up and looked thoughtfully at me. 'Until you start believing it, of course, then you will be down with the organist and his Mafia. What is a Mafia by the way?'

'Actually, I am not absolutely – '

A loud crash interrupted me. It was Reverend Persimmon and Mr Craven entering through the front porch.

3

'Blast!'

Reverend Persimmon nearly always knocks something over when he comes through a door. Then he says, 'Blast!' This time he had bumped into the easel and blackboard that is used to display the excellent pictures produced by the Sunday School children. The easel had entirely collapsed, the blackboard had knocked down a rather tall pile of church magazines, and one picture was almost torn across, while two others floated over the pews to land in the aisle.

'Blast and damn and double-damn and blast!' said Reverend Persimmon. 'Give me a space with no problem in it and I'll guarantee to manufacture one, won't I? Persimmon's got ten minutes of peace available, says Fate, so let's fill it up wth something he never even thought of. Ah! Easel plus boot equals chaos – let's go! What's the matter with this damned easel? It seems to be stuck to the floor!'

Mr Craven, who is a thin, brown, tweedy man with kind, hurt eyes, was quietly picking up the magazines.

'It's many years since I did any physics, Dave,' he said, 'but I'm pretty sure that any attempt to pick up an object that one is standing on is doomed to failure.'

'Blast!' said Reverend Persimmon as he moved his foot and set the easel up again.

'Here are the pictures, Reverend,' I said, holding them out to him. 'We could mend the other one with sellotape, could we not?'

People say a lot of things about our vicar. I once heard Mrs Williams, who does the coffee after church without so much as a thank you, say that he was like an unmade king-size bed that someone had set fire to at one end, and she for one had no intention of getting burned thank you very much, but he has never lost his temper with me and I think he likes me. I do not know why.

'Ah, thank you very much, Hartley old boy,' he said.

'Sorry about all the damning and blasting – been a long day. How are you?'

'I am the most important person in the Church of England,' I announced proudly. 'Nunc told me. Unless I start believing it,' I added, 'then I become like Mr Forsyth.'

'Don't believe it, Hartley, there's a good chap. I couldn't live with two Forsyths, and I'd miss you terribly. Here – you take this picture home and stick it up, you're a whiz-kid at that sort of thing. Come on, Craven, stop messing around with those magazines and help me get some chairs.'

'How fortunate our little flock is,' said Mr Craven as he patted his pile of magazines, 'to have an earthly shepherd in whom qualities of restraint, charity, grace and thankfulness are so evenly distributed.'

'Thinly distributed you mean, don't you? Well, let me tell you, Craven, that those qualities would be pretty thinly distributed in you if you'd had a day like I've just had. It started with the usual loony post.'

'Such as?'

Reverend Persimmon ticked them off on his fingers.

'A communication from some group calling themselves something like "Gay Asthmatic Ember Day Bryanites for Romania", saying that my input was desperately needed –'

'They can't have been called that,' interrupted Mr Craven.

'A letter from that woman with the dog that's supposed to only bark at heretics . . .'

'The one that nearly killed you last time you went round?'

'Yes, that one. A letter from her saying that we should

send all our service books back to the supplier because goodness knows how many opening pages are missing from every single one. And, last but not least, a letter from my bank charging me fifteen pounds for telling me that I owe them fifty quid. Mad!'

Mr Craven and I got five folding chairs from the back of the church, carried them to the space in front of the altar steps, and set them out in a circle. Nunc was sitting on the bottom step, his eyes shut, glowing gently. Reverend Persimmon followed us up the aisle, still talking.

'This afternoon I was visited by a deputation of two, from the "Let's go on being Anglicans but abolish every visible or aural evidence of Anglicanism brigade", saying that we had the wrong sort of Bibles, and why couldn't we get the Living, Throbbing, Slides along the Pew, Opens itself at Random and Points out a Verse Specially for You version. They'd been led to come round, they said, and they kept smiling through gritted teeth and forgiving me for being a spiritual Skoda in the great car park of the church. They were called Nick and Sue, and they were young with very clean necks. Why are they always called Nick and Sue, and why are they always young with very clean necks?'

'You must admit, Dave,' said Mr Craven, who had seated himself on one of the chairs, 'we're not very progressive as a church.'

'What do you mean?'

'Well, we haven't had any splits yet. Aren't they a sign of progress?'

Ignoring what Mr Craven had said, the Vicar sat heavily down on a chair and leaned back with his hands behind his head.

'And just to cap it all, I walk in here quite innocently, and an easel – a demonically possessed easel – flings itself at me and tries to kill me! What a day!'

'A pastoral word for you, Dave.'

'God help us – if he exists – go on then . . .'

Mr Craven suddenly spoke in a loud voice as if he was talking to a big crowd of people.

'In the great motor-race of life, Jesus is the pits!'

I do not always understand Mr Craven and Reverend Persimmon. They both started to laugh extremely loudly.

'Anyway,' said Reverend Persimmon at last, 'it's entrail time. Hartley's the most important person in the Church of England, I don't know what I am any more, and you, Craven, are just a typical, nominal Anglican.'

'Nonsense,' replied Mr Craven, 'I'm a dried out Baptist.'

'And Nunc's asleep,' said the Vicar.

'I am not,' smiled Nunc, opening his eyes and fading gently. 'I have not ceased to incline my ear to you. What is an entrail?'

'Entrails,' answered Reverend Persimmon, speaking more slowly and quietly as he always did when Nunc asked him a question, 'are the bits inside your body that keep it working properly.'

Nunc bounced to his feet and into the remaining chair. He looked like a big marshmallow baby.

'Guts, you mean? Guts are mentioned in one of the books that I have read here, Reverend. I believe they were spilled.'

'Err . . . yes, guts if you like. All I meant was that we're going to look at – talk about – the things that really mean something to us instead of warily analysing some apostrophe in Zephaniah, or agreeing after much deep discussion, that the Resurrection was almost certainly a good thing . . .'

'Is that the form that church discussions generally take?' enquired Nunc in amazement.

'I may have exaggerated a little,' said the Vicar.

'You?' Mr Craven sounded very shocked. 'Surely not!'

'Well, you know what I mean. This group – Nunc and Hartley and you, Craven, and Dot – even though she is so blinking good – where is Dot by the way?'

'She phoned me earlier,' said Mr Craven, 'she'll be a few minutes late. Go on with what you were saying.'

'Well, just that, here, in this group, over the last couple of weeks I've been more able to be me than I have for the last two years, and I don't mean more spiritual. I haven't been spiritual for a long time. I haven't heard from God for a long time. He's been on a long lazy holiday cruise ever since I first came here and had my spiritual vasectomy.'

'Vasectomies are voluntary, Dave,' said Mr Craven gently.

'Not when the choir holds you down and the organist does it, they're not!'

'Do you hate Mr Forsyth, David?' asked Nunc brightly.

Nobody said anything for a few seconds. Sometimes Nunc's questions reminded me of when I had a bad fight with a boy called Richard Simpson who said I was wrong in the head. Right in the middle of us punching each other as hard as we could, out in the yard with the brick floor, Mr Williamson, who was in charge, came out of the back door and emptied a metal bucket of very cold water over our heads. We gasped, and stopped.

'Hate is a very strong word, Nunc,' said Reverend Persimmon at last. He suddenly looked much more upset than angry.

'It describes a very strong feeling,' put in Mr Craven. 'If that's what you feel, then that's what you feel. They don't perform surgery on your anger glands at ordination, do they? Come clean! It'll be good for you.'

'You can talk, Craven,' replied the Vicar, raising his voice and turning his head to glare at the man beside him. 'You're not exactly an open book, are you?'

'Pages haven't even been snipped, Dave,' said Mr Craven. 'I write fantasy and hide from reality. But,' he added, almost whispering, 'I do have a combined honours degree in Friendship and Hypocrisy.'

Reverend Persimmon peered into Mr Craven's face for a moment, silently mouthing the last few words that had been said, then he swung away and leaned his head right back, so that he was looking up towards the big dark beams in the ceiling.

'This year,' he announced in the sort of voice that newsreaders use, 'the president of the Christian Cowards Liberation Movement will be the Reverend David Persimmon, who shows exactly what he's thinking and feeling, but hasn't got the plain, ordinary guts – '

'Or entrails,' suggested Nunc interestedly.

'He hasn't got the entrails to put a name to it in case the last little bit of vicar inside him runs away in horror, leaving him with the realization that he might as well go and be a greengrocer . . .'

At last there was a chance for me to say something.

'I used to help at a greengrocer's, Reverend Persimmon.'

'And when you were doing that, Hartley, did you do things with cabbages and beans and carrots and apples?'

'And potatoes, yes.'

The Vicar stopped looking at the ceiling. Instead he leaned right forward and stared at the bit of floor between his feet.

'Potatoes, of course. And when you went home afterwards, did you say, "I've been moving potatoes, and piling up cabbages, and putting carrots in bags, and polishing apples, and sorting out beans, but I *haven't* been helping at the greengrocers"?'

'Of course not, because I *had* been helping at the greengrocer's.'

'Hartley,' he said very quietly, 'you're a better man than I . . .'

Suddenly the Vicar shot to his feet, strode across the front of the church, and leapt up the steps into the pulpit. Leaning forward with his hands clamped to the narrow wooden shelf in front of him he looked from one side of the church to the other and back again, as if every single pew was crammed with people (which they never are).

'Yes!' he said, in a very large voice. 'Damn and blast and triple blast and double damn – yes!! I hate and dread and fear and detest and despise every molecule, every neutron, every proton, every electron that exists in his loathesome body! From the moment he first fixed me with that sardonic gaze of his and informed me that the St Wilfred's boat was fitted with stabilizers so efficient that no one had succeeded in rocking it yet, I have been a jelly in his presence, an inedible and flavourless jelly. If Nigel Forsyth is going to hell, then I want to go to heaven. If he has a room booked in Paradise then please let me sink gently into Hades, or the General Synod or Bognor – or anywhere where he is not. He brings all the devils of my childhood chattering out of their nasty little hiding places, accusing and prodding and diminishing with their horrible pointed tongues and their rancid bad-memory breaths!

' "Thought you'd got rid of daddy, didn't you? He's back! Called Forsyth now – screw your insides up just like before, till you start baby-moaning inside . . ."

' "Thought you'd tied up all the loose ends, did you? Wrong!"

' "Thought you could leave that pathetic little boy behind in the back room listening to his world falling apart on the other side of the door, did you? He's found you, he's caught up with you, he's in you, he *is* you . . ." '

I had never seen a vicar cry before, and perhaps I never will again, but that night Reverend Persimmon did not just cry, he sobbed and sobbed and sobbed over the front edge of the pulpit, hanging down like a huge rag doll. And then a very peculiar thing happened. Mind you, peculiar things often happened during that time when Nunc was with us. That was one of the reasons why I liked Thursday evenings so much. Anything could happen.

What happened this time was that the light I had turned on when I came into the church started to go out, but gradually, as if it was on one of those dimmer-switches that I was talking about earlier. None of *us* did it. Dot Jenkins had slipped in through the back way while the Vicar was crying, but she was already sitting in the circle with us when the light started fading, so it was definitely nothing to do with her.

As the light over our heads got dimmer and dimmer, the

gleam inside Nunc grew brighter and brighter, until his soft white glow was the only light in the church. It made me feel as though we were sitting by a street lamp on a snowy night, except that I felt very warm and safe as well.

The second peculiar thing was that Reverend Persimmon stopped crying and stood up very straight in the pulpit.

I cannot have been the only one who thought he was looking intently at someone or something at the back of the church, because Dot, Mr Craven and I all turned our heads in that direction at the same time. There was nobody there, but the Vicar started to speak in a sad, slow voice, his eyes wide open and full of wetness, and I am quite sure he was not speaking to any of us. His words came out in lines, like those poems that do not rhyme, as we sat very still and listened:

> Poor sad child,
> Poor child,
> Poor boy,
> Don't run – don't run away,
> Don't hide.
> I love you.
> I am sorry that I let you down,
> I left you,
> I settled for too little,
> I was frightened of your pain.
> Pain is better buried.
> I was wrong
> To leave you there,
> Leave you wondering if tears can ever really dry.
> I threw my lot in with the half-alive

But now,
Now I've come to find you,
I can face you now,
I so long to see your face,
I want to see you smile,
See you smile, dear child,
Be my child again.
I've brought a friend,
A friend who changes things.
He's with me now,
His name,
His name is Jesus –
Jesus.
He can heal you,
He can make you smile again,
You'll love him,
I love him,
He loves you
So much,
So much,
Poor sad child.

Dot Jenkins is very old and stiff in her joints, but as the electric light came on again and Nunc's snowy brightness faded away, she left her chair, climbed slowly up the pulpit steps and laid a hand on the Vicar's arm. He jumped and turned round when she touched him, as though he had just woken up.

'Hello, Dot,' he said, 'where did you spring from? And where did all that come from? And who am I? And lots of other questions . . .'

'Come and sit down, David.' She sounded like one of

my teachers when I was very little – cheerful and strong. 'I fear, David,' she said, 'that you are faced, once again, with the possibility that there may be a god after all.'

'Ah, Dot my darling,' answered Reverend Persimmon wearily, as he followed her back down the steps, 'I'm only a nominal atheist you know. The hound of heaven is always nipping at my heels.'

'He'll bite your bottom one of these days,' said Mr Craven, 'then you'll scream "Hallelujah!" in top C. Are you feeling all right, Dave? That was wonderful, what you said up there. Sit down. Sit down, Dot.'

'It may have been wonderful,' replied the Vicar, 'but I'm not sure who said it. Nunc?'

'Yes, David.' Nunc was very calm and still.

'Nunc, you asked me just now if I hate Forsyth.'

'I did.'

'Well, I do. It's complicated by all sorts of other things, but I do hate him. He's my enemy.'

'How pleasant for him,' said Nunc.

'Pleasant?' Dot sounded shocked.

'Yes indeed, Dot. I imagine that Mr Forsyth has been moved in sundry places by David's great generosity and kindness towards him, and, if he did but know it, has greatly benefited from the prayers that his brother offers unceasingly on his behalf.'

'I see.' Dot smiled and nodded.

Reverend Persimmon rubbed his hands all over his face and through his thick red hair.

'Nunc,' he said, 'what are you talking about?'

'Perhaps I have misunderstood,' replied Nunc calmly, 'but your writings include a direct commandment to love your enemies and pray for those who use you badly. And, in another place, are you not instructed to invite to your home those whom you do not wish to invite to your home? I assumed that Mr Forsyth must have eaten with you on many occasions.'

'Invite that man to dinner? I'd rather – '

'Rather not do what Jesus specifically commands?' interrupted Dot.

'It seems to me,' continued Nunc, 'that if I were a member of this Church of England, I might say to a man or woman, "Prove you hate me by loving me. Prove you disagree with me by using my ideas. Prove I am your enemy by treating me like a friend. Prove that you don't want me inside your life by inviting me to dinner."'

Mr Craven smiled. 'It's a very fine ideal, Nunc, but can you imagine the effect if everyone did it? Dot comes up to me one day, smiles, and says, "Richard, I would be so pleased if you were able to dine with me next Friday." "Oh!" I respond, "so that's what you think of me, is it? What have I ever done to you to deserve this sort of treatment? I suppose you've been praying for me as well! So much for friendship!"'

'Richard,' said Dot sweetly.

'Yes, Dot?'

'Don't be silly, dear.'

'Ground-glass sandwiches, arsenic cocktail, and a few little cyanide fancies – that should just about do it,' said the Vicar in a practical sort of voice.

'Do what?' asked Dot.

'I should imagine,' said Mr Craven, 'that the holy father here is organizing a menu for his meal with the organist.'

'Why don't you invite him to dinner, David?' Dot sounded as if she had made up her mind. 'Try a little obedience, as Nunc suggested, and see what comes of it. Eh? What do you think?'

Reverend Persimmon sat and stared into the distance for a few minutes, his lips compressed tightly like a stubborn little boy.

'The other day,' he said eventually, 'Stanley Carstairs, who sings in the choir and has all five feet in different camps, was kind enough to tell me – because he thought I ought to know, you understand – that Nigel Forsyth had told him a joke about me. Apparently Forsyth said that he had discovered a verse in the Old Testament that prophesied the Reverend Persimmon's coming to St Wilfred's.'

There was quite a long silence, then Mr Craven reached over to a pew and picked up a church Bible.

'The reference, Dave?' he asked.

'The reference is Jonah, chapter four, verse seven,' answered the Vicar in a very serious voice. 'By all means read it out Craven, but if you so much as titter, I shall proceed to demonstrate an involuntary what-we-were-talking-about-before-Dot-came on your person, using a blunt pair of scissors that are very handy, just over there in the vestry. Do I make myself clear?'

'Crystal clear, Dave,' said Mr Craven as he leafed through the Bible, 'now, let me see . . . chapter four, verse seven. Here we are . . .' He hesitated.

'Well, go on then!' snapped the Vicar. 'What are you waiting for?'

'The Lord appointed a worm,' read Mr Craven loudly and clearly.

Reverend Persimmon glared at us one by one to see if we were laughing. Mr Craven did not even smile, Nunc looked rather puzzled, Dot looked quite cross, but I have to confess that when the Vicar looked at me I burst into laughter, even though I didn't want to. I was so frightened!

'Please forgive me, Reverend Persimmon,' I spluttered, 'I did not mean to laugh! It was just that you are so much *not* like a worm, and I . . .'

Instead of getting angry with me, the Vicar started to laugh as well, and so did all the others, so I just joined in. I do not think I shall ever understand people.

'Anyway,' said the Vicar, 'that's how he makes me feel – like a worm, weak and wriggly. He's a great, strong mistle-thrush.' He looked round at us all again. 'Do you really think I ought to ask him to dinner?'

'Of course,' said Nunc simply, 'endue him plenteously with gifts.'

'It would be a beginning,' added Dot, 'and it would certainly surprise him.'

Mr Craven said, 'Go for it, Dave. I'll come and hold your hand if you want. In fact, I'll cook the meal if you like. Making the poor man eat something you've cooked would be an act of blatant aggression.'

'Thanks, Dick, I'll take you up on that. Hartley, what do you think? Should I invite Mr Forsyth to dinner, or not?'

I was very unsure about what to say for a second. People do not usually want to know what I think about anything. But Dot knows secret things sometimes. And Nunc certainly did. If they thought it was a good idea then it must be.

'Yes,' I said, remembering something someone said in an old adventure story, 'the notion is an exceedingly fine one. I applaud it.'

Reverend Persimmon chuckled when I said that, and Dot leaned towards me and whispered, 'Very well put, Hartley, very well put indeed.' That was nice.

'Well,' said the Vicar, 'that settles it. I shall invite my beloved brother to a sumptuous repast next week, and I shall report back to you all the week after next and tell you how wrong you were.'

4

Nunc said, 'Tell me, what exactly is a vasect – '

'Aliens don't need 'em,' interrupted Mr Craven hastily. 'Nunc, earlier on we were talking about who we are, or what we are. Dave said he didn't know what *he* was, he said I was a nominal Anglican, and Hartley was the most important person in the Church of England (which is almost certainly true, in my view). You weren't here then, were you, Dot? What are you?'

'What am I?' repeated Dot, a little flustered. 'Well, I'm lots of things, I suppose. An eighty-year-old nuisance to some people, as I am perfectly aware. I have never been able to tell anything but the truth. That is not a virtue, it is simply a form of training.'

Mr Craven sucked air in through pursed lips. 'Oh, Dot, you know as well as I do that there's always a problem when truth starts creeping into Christianity. Why can't you be good, and collude like all the others?'

Dot is very pretty even though she is terribly old, but when Mr Craven said that, she sat up straight in her chair and looked at him with a very cross face indeed.

'I will not collude with nonsense!' she said. 'I will not pretend something has happened because somebody's private little spiritual edifice might develop cracks if I don't! Nor will I, under any circumstances, deny the love and forgiveness and grace that I have found in Jesus. I promised my earthly father seventy years ago, and my heavenly father fifty-five years ago, that I would always endeavour to be true to myself. I have failed, of course, because I am a weak human being, but I renew my promise daily, and I trust that the Lord will uphold me when I stand, and forgive me when I fall. Far too many people fall away from the faith because they suddenly become aware that their religious lives have largely consisted of collusion – yes, collusion, Richard – in regular corporate acts of dishonesty. When religious optimism takes the place of spiritual reality there is bound to be trouble – bound to be trouble!'

I would have felt quite squashed, I believe, if Dot had answered me so fiercely, but Mr Craven just listened with his head on one side and a funny smile in his eyes.

'Corporate acts of dishonesty, eh?' He nodded slowly. 'Are you talking about the sort of churches where they think that liturgy is something you get from the Indian take-away?'

The Vicar snorted agreement. 'The sort of church,' he added, 'where they think a rood-screen is a device that you watch blue movies on?'

'No, indeed, I do not refer to any specific denominational group,' said Dot, still very fiercely. 'As you well know – both of you – I regularly attend a mid-week worship meeting arranged by the House Church that uses the junior school in Bowden Road. The uninhibited

quality of that meeting is a complement and' – she fixed
the Vicar with a very sharp eye – 'something of an antidote
to most of the services that I attend at St Wilfred's.'

The Vicar made a noise as though he had been shot,
clamped his hand over his heart, and pretended to fall off
his chair. Dot did not take any notice.

'The Anglican church,' she continued, 'is as guilty as
any other group. In fact, if we are descending into
flippancy, I might point out that there is biblical support
for the view that Anglicans will arrive in heaven before
anyone else.'

'They will?' asked Mr Craven.

'Scripture tells us that the dead will rise first.'

'You made a joke, Dot!' said Reverend Persimmon.
'Let me be the first to congratulate you on attempting
something so radical at such a late stage in life. Truly
wonderful!'

Dot could not help smiling. 'I shall certainly not
attempt to do such a thing again,' she said. 'I know I
sounded a little preachy and serious just now, but I meant
everything I said. As for the business about Anglicans –
well, what does it mean when you say you're an Anglican
nowadays?'

'Is an Anglican the same as a Christian?' asked Nunc,
who had been listening quietly.

'Anglicans *can* be Christians,' said the Vicar slowly.

'And Christians *can* certainly be Anglicans,' contributed Mr Craven.

'But not all Anglicans *are* Christians,' frowned Dot.

'And Christians are by no means all Anglicans,' added
Reverend Persimmon.

'An Anglican can be renewed,' said Dot.

'Like a library book?' I asked. That made them all laugh, but I am not sure why.

'Or, he can be like the Vicar,' said Mr Craven.

'If you're not careful, Craven,' said Reverend Persimmon, 'I shall tell Nunc what you said the other day when Angus Wattle's house group came back from the conference in Brighton and led the mid-week meeting as though they'd all been fitted with new batteries.'

Mr Craven shrugged. 'I shall stand by whatever I said.' His brows knitted. 'What the hell *did* I say?'

'You said, and I quote: "This is the way the world ends, not with a bang but a Whimber." Correct?'

'Well, yes, I did say something like that,' agreed Mr Craven lazily, 'but those who know me well –'

'Us, you mean?' interrupted Dot.

'Those who know me well are quite aware that I am a closet charismatic, which, unless I am very much mistaken, is precisely in line with the recommendations of the apostle Paul in the first book of Corinthians.'

'I think you *are* very much mistaken, Richard,' said Dot. 'Paul did not suggest that you should keep all your gifts hidden in a closet at home, and never bring them to church. I think' – she spoke very kindly – 'that you are frightened of being as vulnerable as David was just now. Am I right?'

Mr Craven's face seemed to close up when Dot said that. I usually like his face, but now it was hard and locked and cold. He stood up and walked slowly down the aisle with his hands in his pockets, until he was nearly invisible in the shadows. Then he turned round and spoke quietly, but very clearly.

'I don't like being bullied, Dot,' he said. 'I am what I

am, and whatever I am is inside me and has nothing to do with anyone else. I don't mind jokes and I don't mind other people doing whatever they think is a good idea for them, but I only joined this group because I thought I wouldn't be got at. So don't get at me! Understand?'

Dot was nearly in tears.

'Richard, I'm sorry, I really didn't mean –'

'I remember that meeting!'

Nunc's voice rang through the church like a chime of bells, interrupting the atmosphere and making us all look at him instead of Mr Craven.

'What meeting, Nunc?' asked the Vicar.

'The one where the people had the new batteries,' said Nunc excitedly. 'I remember it – I remember the two notes. It was the first time I had heard them sounding together since I left – since I left the place where I was. I have been taught to accept all things as may be most expedient to me, but on that day another tear was added to the bottle that is kept for me in my home, and I felt cut down like a flower . . .'

I really did not understand what Nunc was talking about, but he looked so like a sad, white teddy bear as he sat with his head on one side and his hands on his knees that I almost went over to cuddle him. I think I would have done if the Vicar had not broken the silence that followed Nunc's speech.

'What do you mean by these two notes, Nunc? The music was a bit more frenetic – I mean, lively – but other than that . . .'

'Would you like to hear them?' Nunc sat up straight, his eyes shining.

Reverend Persimmon, Dot and I looked at each other

(Mr Craven was still somewhere back in the shadows). None of us plays any musical instrument, and as for Nunc, well, I suppose he might have been able to play a harmonica or some other small instrument, but his legs were far too small to reach the pedals of an organ, and that was the only musical thing in the church.

'We would very much like to hear them, Nunc,' said Dot politely. She turned towards the back of the church. 'Richard, won't you come and . . . ?'

'Come on, Craven!' said the Vicar. 'Stop your tantrum and sit down again. You can put your entrails away – we don't want to see 'em.'

I held my breath, but Mr Craven came back up the aisle looking weary, though smiling again, thank goodness. He walked up to Dot, put his hands on her shoulders and bent to kiss her cheek.

'Sorry, Dot, the old guard went down there for a minute.'

'No, I'm sorry, Richard,' she patted his hand. 'I'm so busy being truthful I forget to be sensitive.'

'This is all very touching,' said Reverend Persimmon, 'but when you've finished forgiving and apologizing and weeping all over each other, Nunc's got something he wants us to hear. All yours, Nunc.'

Nunc left his chair, climbed the steps and stood in front of the altar, eyes closed and arms outstretched on either side.

Then it started.

At first it was not a noise at all. It was more like a vibration right inside the walls and pillars and floor, as though there were big engines buried in the stone and wood around us. I am not sure how the others felt, and I know it sounds very silly, but it seemed to me that the whole building was suddenly not heavy at all. Then the noise began, a deep rumbling snore of a noise, all on one note and quite nice at first, a little bit like when I used to sit on top of the old-fashioned spin-drier at Dalton House when I was very little. But after a minute or two it was so heavy and unchanging and unstoppable that all of us put our hands over our ears to make it go away. It was powerful but dead.

It was like a dream after that. Nunc lifted his hands high above his head, and another note, a sweet, high, flute-like noise filled the church, mixing with the lower one to produce a sound that made you want to weep as soon as you heard it. It was like so *many* things, that I made a list afterwards.

It was like the end of a beautiful piece of music.
Like waking after a nightmare.
Like laughing when the pain has gone.
Like finding a light-switch in the dark.
Like an ice-cold drink on a hot day.
Like suddenly knowing you are loved.
Like perfect weather.
Like the happy ending of a film that made you cry.
Like finishing a jig-saw puzzle.
Like knowing that *everything* will be looked after and sorted out.
Like discovering that someone *was* in charge all the time.
Like peace.

As the sound died away we all sat like statues, as if a

magician had touched us with a wand. I did not realize that Nunc was back in his chair until he spoke.

'Like that,' he said happily.

Reverend Persimmon looked like a man who has been hit very hard on the head with a brick.

'That was awfully real, Nunc,' he said weakly. 'I don't actually remember that happening in the service led by the people with new batteries.'

'I do,' said Nunc, 'but I think my ears are made differently from yours, and in any case,' he smiled round at us contentedly, 'as many as are here present were able to hear the two notes tonight.'

'Nunc,' said Mr Craven, 'what was that deep, bass note?'

'It was a deep bass note,' said Nunc, clearly puzzled.

Mr Craven screwed up his face and shifted position in his chair. 'Yes, I know it was what it *was*, but – I mean – what did it signify? What did it mean?'

'It meant what has been,' said Nunc, 'what has been earned, what has been bought, what has been laid down, what has been prepared.'

There was a pause. Reverend Persimmon opened his mouth and shut it again.

'And the high note?' asked Mr Craven.

'The now, life, what is, who is, what will be, eternity.'

'The one is monotonous, the other is shrill, but together they are beautiful?' suggested the Vicar.

Nunc nodded enthusiastically, and the Vicar clasped his hands above his head like a victorious boxer.

'I got something right, Craven! Did you hear that? I got something right! There's hope for me yet.'

'I was at that service,' breathed Dot, who had hardly

moved since the harmony died away. 'I loved it, and – you asked me just now, Richard, what I *am*, didn't you?'

Mr Craven nodded.

'Well,' went on Dot, 'I certainly did not hear that beautiful sound, but – '

'Nor did I,' I said.

'But I felt a little – just a little – of the feeling that we experienced just now. And I think that, right at the centre, it was all about Jesus. So, if you ask me what I am, I suppose the answer is – well, does anyone mind if I use a slang term?'

'The slangier the better, Dot!' said the Vicar, 'but keep it clean for Craven's sake. He's a delicate soul.'

5

'I have a nephew,' said Dot, 'my youngest brother Jonathan's boy. His name is Philip and he really is quite a delightful young man, although he does tease me terribly at times. Anyway, he is an officer in the Royal Navy, and last month he brought me a book of naval slang terms, saying that he felt it was "just my sort of reading". In fact, as the naughty boy knew perfectly well' – Dot flushed slightly – 'some of the phrases and expressions included in the book were decidedly off-colour.'

'Such as?'

'However,' continued Dot, ignoring the Vicar, 'there was one phrase that intrigued me greatly. I am not mechanically inclined, but I understand from this section of the book that the rotor-blades on top of naval helicopters are attached to the body of the machine by a nut which is colloquially known as the "Jesus Nut".'

'Why the *Jesus* Nut?' asked Mr Craven.

'It is known as the Jesus Nut,' explained Dot, 'because if you fly a helicopter without ensuring that this nut is sufficiently tightened, you will probably meet him! I find the picture a helpful one. I think – I hope that I am a Jesus Nut. Having said that, though, I do become very confused at times about my role in the church.'

'Huh!' exploded Reverend Persimmon, 'wait till you're a Vicar!'

'How long do you suppose I shall have to wait for that?' enquired Dot, her eyes twinkling.

'In my job,' said the Vicar, 'you have to be an accountant, a diplomat, a preacher, a chairman, a hospital visitor, a writer, a taxi-driver, a public speaker, a counsellor, a chair arranger, an organist feeder, and err . . . a giver-out of crèche helmets to the children's workers. Fancy my job, Craven?'

Mr Craven did not laugh – or even smile.

'I feel a bit crushed by this evening, Dave,' he said. 'I don't know if I have a role at all. Professional pessimist perhaps.' He looked around the church. 'People say these are some of the finest stained-glass windows in England, but, to me, even the angels look as if they've got fowlpest. I think I'm frightened of being happy. But I'd like – I dunno – I'd like to be something useful.'

'Well, in that case, Dick,' the Vicar leaned over and punched Mr Craven on the shoulder, 'why don't you get your biro out and write something for *us* – for the church?'

'Nothing to say really – not yet. Besides – '

Nunc said, 'I greatly desire a shawm, or a sackbut would do.'

'Well, that's a conversation stopper,' laughed Reverend Persimmon. 'Why?'

'In order to show myself joyful before the Lord, the King,' replied Nunc, 'to express thankfulness for the story that Richard is about to tell us.'

We all looked at Mr Craven. His eyebrows shot up so far that they almost disappeared under his hair.

'Story?' He scratched the very top of his head with the very tip of his finger. 'I can't get any ideas for my own stuff at the moment, let alone moral tales for the brethren.'

'I should tell it from the lectern,' suggested Nunc helpfully. 'Is it about people not being satisfied with what they are?'

'It isn't about anything because it doesn't exist,' said Mr Craven wildly. 'I don't know what you're talking about!'

'I think it would come over well from the lectern, Nunc, you're absolutely right. D'you agree, Dot?'

Dot nodded worriedly.

'Hartley?' The Vicar was asking me now.

I noticed that Nunc was starting to glow again, and somehow I knew that there *was* going to be a story.

'Yes,' I said. I cleared my throat. 'I think that if you were to station yourself behind the lectern, Mr Craven, you would be able to tell us an excellent story.'

I think Mr Craven had been about to say something very angry indeed, but after I had spoken he sat perfectly still for a short time with his hands flat on his knees, then he stood up and walked very slowly across to the lectern with a big brass eagle on top and, leaning across it, said, 'Sure about this, Hartley?'

'Oh, yes,' I said, horribly unsure now, 'an excellent story . . .'

Mr Craven lifted his eyes up towards the big painted organ pipes at the back of the church, sighed a very deep sigh, then letting his hands hang down over the front of the lectern with his fingers loosely intertwined, he began to tell us a story.

It was midnight in the psalm-soft darkness of the parish church, a church that was not unlike this one. Only the faintest glow from a streetlight outside filtered through the tinted glass of a window in the south wall. There was just enough light to avoid bumping into things – if there had been anyone there to do the bumping, that is. The overhead projector was complaining again.

'I don't want to be an overhead projector! I never did want to be an overhead projector! I don't feel like an overhead projector! Every time I'm switched on and the power floods through me, I feel as if I'm going to do something great – something wonderful! And what do I *actually* do? What is thrown up onto that great, blank, white stupid screen over there whenever some grubby acetate has been slapped unceremoniously over my face?'

'I like being a screen,' interrupted the screen, his voice muffled because he was tightly rolled up.

'I'll tell you what's thrown up,' continued the overhead projector. 'It's either a selection of the curate's appallingly drawn stick-people with totally unconvincing backgrounds, or a succession of those dreadful cowboy songs that pass for music in this church nowadays.'

'Are your acetates grubby?' intoned the pulpit in a

deep mock-parsonical voice, 'I know mine are.' The pulpit fancied himself as something of a satirist.

'Can't see what's the matter with you,' muttered the font stonily. 'At least there's no controversy about your use. I've spent nine hundred and fifty years doubting the theological validity of my own function. Imagine that!

'Anyway,' he asked, 'what do you *want* to be?'

There was a pause. Last week's flowers, looking for a little excitement before they died, whispered, 'Tell us! Tell us!'

The overhead projector spoke with passionate intensity and yearning: 'I want to be an organ – that's what I really want. That's what I dream of all the time. I want to send thundering, awe-inspiring chords reverberating through the building, from the bottom of the deepest foundations to the highest point on the tower. I want to move people to tears of joy and repentance! I want – '

'I hate to disillusion you,' said the organ, his voice a poem in mellow cello, 'but when you have accompanied this congregation as they sing "Give Me Oil In My Lamp" at snail's pace for the ninety-third time, with the Vicar's utilitarian baritone leading the way like a one-legged blind sherpa, you forget all about thunderous chords or moving people to tears, I can assure you. Besides, it's all guitars and metallophones nowadays, often played by people who find it difficult to believe that there are more than three chords in the universe.'

'I'm sick of being a paving slab,' came a rather flat voice from the floor of the aisle.

'You mustn't let people walk all over you,' called a three-year-old copy of the *Church Times*, and a chorus of Anglican mirth rang and fluttered and resounded through the nocturnal solemnity of St Vernon's. But the nightly complaints of the overhead projector were beginning to affect everybody. Fifty wooden voices rang out in dark-stained harmony:

'We refuse
To be the pews
We'll deal with minds
And not behinds'

'Let's all alter!' said the altar.

'Wouldn't say no to a little change,' rattled the collection plate.

'I want to ring Mr Cuthbertson!' boomed the largest bell in the belfry.

'I want to be used again!' squeaked a desperately shabby little sixteen sixty-two prayer book. 'Use me! Use me! Use me in a sketch about me being useless. Use me as literature. Use me for a paper-chase. Just *use* me!'

'I can't stand the responsibility of being the P.C.C.'s *raison d'être*,' moaned the heating system. 'I want to be a spiritual issue. I want to radiate joy.'

'I like being a screen,' repeated the same muffled voice as before. 'I like rolling down and I like people looking at me.'

'I want to be a lectern!' barked a Victorian brass plaque.

'That'll be a lesson for you,' cried the rather toffee-beaked eagle.

'I want to be somebody's well-thumbed pocket edition,' said the huge, brass-clasped church Bible, sadly.

'I want to travel,' bleated a tiny, pocket-size Gideon New Testament, 'and stay in posh hotels.'

'Just a minute!' shouted the overhead projector. 'You don't understand! You've got it all wrong! It's *me* who wants to change. I'm the one who said it first. I want all of you to stay the same – it makes me feel safe. I never intended – '

A hymn of protest drowned the rest of his comments. St Vernon's was in utter chaos.

'Good heavens!' whispered one unsold church magazine to another, 'It's a good job the humans don't go on like this. They'd never get anything done . . .'

When the story had ended we all clapped, including Nunc, and Mr Craven went from the lectern to the top of the steps to take a little bow. When he was back in his chair he turned to Nunc, and said, 'Well?'

'Just another short cut,' said Nunc, looking more like a little child than ever. 'Is it nearly time for a drink now?'

'I'll go and put the kettle on,' said Dot.

6

Later that evening, when I arrived home, Mrs Bletchley made me a cup of hot chocolate in the kitchen, and asked me how my evening had gone.

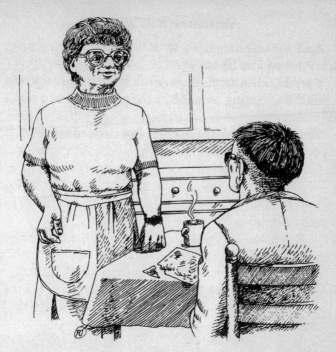

'It was extremely interesting and unusual, thank you very much, Mrs Bletchley,' I replied. 'Nunc said that I was the most important person in the Church of England, although I don't think I am, so I might be; the Vicar told us about his vasectomy and cried, then talked to an invisible boy when Nunc glowed; Mr Craven was cross when he thought he was being got at; Nunc made a beautiful noise that was like ever so many different things; Dot told us that she was a Jesus nut: and Mr Craven found that he *did* know a story about an overhead projector who wanted to be an organ, and then we had drinks . . . Oh, and I've brought back this picture to mend. Reverend Persimmon tore it when he knocked the easel over and said "Blast!"'

'And this all happened at St Wilfred's this evening, dear?' asked Mrs Bletchley.

'Yes,' I said, 'our meetings are quite exciting nowadays. I think that having an alien in the group makes a lot of difference.'

'Yes, dear,' said Mrs Bletchley in a rather faint voice, 'I suppose it probably would.'

Part Three
Dot's Account

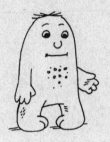

Dot's Account

1

I was deeply moved and profoundly impressed by Hartley's account of the evening when Nunc allowed us to hear that wonderfully harmonious sound that our ears are not normally attuned to. Hartley's scrupulous memory for detail omitted nothing of importance, including my own arrogance and insensitivity towards dear Richard Craven, who quite rightly objected to being 'got at'. I really should try very hard to avoid sounding as stern and religious as I must have done on that occasion. I was very pleased, though, to learn that Hartley regards me as being pretty, even if I am terribly old!

That evening remains in my memory also because it was on the following Sunday that David Persimmon's preaching underwent a change that was as sudden as it was unsubtle. Despite his protestations to the contrary, I knew in the depths of my heart that David was a child of God and a follower of Jesus, and I had been hoping and praying ever since his arrival at St Wilfred's that he would learn to love and forgive himself sufficiently to reveal his heart to the congregation. His sermons, until the Sunday in question, had been strangely formal and uninspired for a man who at times was capable of such explosive behaviour. Once, in the course of a very small dinner party at my flat in Varney Court, I truly believed that the Vicar might alter his attitude to preaching when Richard delivered a mock sermon in, as he put it, 'the true Persimmon style'.

Richard has supplied me with a copy of this very well observed caricature, and I trust that David will not object to its inclusion here.

May the weight of my hips and the combination of all our parts be acceptable in thy diet, oh, Lord our mumble, mumble.

Dreary beloved, tonight I would like to share with you a portion of scripture that has always meant a tremendous amount to me, and I hope, from the heart of my bottom, that it will mean as much, in the fullness of time, to all of you, and perhaps some of those who are not here tonight, but who will, doubtless, receive an account of what has been said, from those of you who are err . . . present to hear it.

This portion is taken from what I always call the gynaecological letter, Paul's epistle to the Fallopians. We are told in the fifteenth chapter of the twentieth book about one little group of believers, that, and I quote: 'They went down.' Wonderful words – they went down. They went *down*. They didn't go up, as I think many of us would have been very tempted to do in their place. No, they went down. They descended: they moved from up here, to down there: they started at the top – and they ended at the bottom: if you like, they reversed the direction of their perpendicular motion: one could almost say that they changed their altitude: they went down.

My wife and I have an old and dear friend, a very dear friend, called Steve. Steve and I trained at St Yorick's together during the war, under little more than a skeleton staff. He was a bit of a church history expert, and I used to do pretty well in the 'Keeping-your-teeth-clenched-together-when-you-speak' classes. And, as I said, Steve is a dear, dear friend, a dear friend, stays with us frequently for long periods, very dear friend – very expensive. And old Steve, you know, he's his own man, very adventurous for an Anglican. For instance, when he stays with us, he always likes to use the guest room – it's just his way. And you can always tell when old Steve's up in the morning because he comes out of his room! He's got a sort of pattern – amuses my wife and me no end – out of his room, into the bathroom, back to his room again and down to breakfast.

Conformist? No!

Lovable? Well, no, not really, just expensive.

Anyway, on this particular morning, old Steve went through the first part of this rather eccentric routine of his, and he set off along the landing – that's Steve's way of getting to the stairs – and yet again it was possible to see how things dovetail together in an extraordinary way whenever err . . . they do. Just at the top of the stairs was a little wooden train (probably left there by my son, Tommy, who'd been playing with it just before going to work). So, along comes old Steve, miles away as usual and, my goodness, did he catch that train! The eight thirty-five non-stop express to Downstairsland.

There was a terrific crash as Steve landed in the hall. I won't tell you which part of his anatomy he landed on – let's just say that he made maximus use of his gluteous. Ha-ha-ha!

After that, of course, everything went mad. But,

you know, in the midst of the telephone calls, and the ambulance siren, and Steve's piteous cries as he was taken off to the Accident and Emergency Unit in the next town but three, I realized that there was a lesson here for all of us.

When old Steve's foot hit that wooden engine, what did he do? Well, in a very real sense, he went down. He went down!

He inadvertently embraced gravitation.

He surrendered his elevation.

He eschewed upwardness.

He abandoned the high ground.

Like a spiritual Eddie Edwards he plummeted like a dead eagle to the point of his destiny – he went down!

And what of us? Are we ready to go down, despite the fact that all those around us are going up? Let's decide that, when it's our turn to go, the same will be said of us as is inscribed on old Steve's memorial plaque: HE WENT DOWN. Amen.

And now we sing number one thousand, nine hundred and forty-three in *Hymns – Prehistoric and Ancient*, one of those truly wonderful old favourites that still have something very special to say to us in this age:

Forswear, through strait vain faith doth flee
And whilst betimes with cherubim
Redemption's law vouchsafeth be
Much less availeth now for him.

All together now! . . .

At first, it seemed that Richard's humorous ploy had made a real impact on David. He sat very quietly for a time after laughing quite immoderately, especially at Richard's ridiculous hymn verse. Then he began to speak in a low but extremely serious voice.

'Craven,' he said, 'that was very amusing, but it also forced me to think about my own preaching. As I sat here listening just now I remembered something in my childhood that probably – well, probably contributed a lot to the problems I have now. Can I tell you about it?'

So gratified was I by this sign of apparent vulnerability in David that I completely forgot the ludicrously childish game that Richard and he indulge in periodically. It consists of one of them initiating a conversation that is ostensibly serious, but culminates in some foolish absurdity. On this occasion Richard was quite taken in.

'Yes, Dave,' he said. 'Look, I didn't mean to really upset you with that stuff. I was just – '

David waved his hand dismissively. 'No, no, Dick, it's all right about that. It's just this – this memory that surfaced.'

He paused, the pungency of his feelings seeming to overwhelm him temporarily. He looked appealingly into his friend's eyes.

'Go on, Dave,' said Richard, 'we're listening.'

'Well,' said David, twisting his fingers together nervously as he spoke, 'when I was a kid we didn't have much money at home. We always ate enough, but things were tight – very tight. We lived in the north-west and we got an awful lot of rain for most of the year. Dad did his best, but it just wasn't possible to get coats for all of us kids.

'There was this boy at school, Robert Dunning he was called, who came to school one day with a brand new waterproof coat. It was red and blue – I remember that – and it was everything I'd always wanted and could never have. And over the next few months I became – ' he stopped and swallowed hard ' – I became really obsessed about the whole thing. I know you must think it sounds so idiotic . . .'

He gazed at each of us in turn, his eyes like those of a dumb animal in pain. We shook our heads solemnly and said, 'Oh, no, of course not . . .'

'I dreamed day and night about that red and blue coat,' went on the Vicar, obviously reassured. 'I stood outside clothes shops and pressed my nose against the glass, longing to have a new coat of my own. In the end my mother got really worried and took me along to the doctor. She told him that – well, you know – that all I thought and talked about was waterproof coats, and after he'd asked a few questions, he said – '

David buried his face in his hands, his shoulders heaving with emotion. I placed an encouraging hand on his arm. Controlling himself, he looked up once more.

'He said I was anoraksic!'

I cannot begin to express the annoyance that I felt, and feel, over idiocies of this kind, but I must admit that Richard took it in good part, merely threatening to 'get his own back' as soon as possible. Sadly, though, David's sermons did not improve as a result of Richard's parody.

However, as I have already said, on the Sunday following the meeting that Hartley described, something quite new happened in the pulpit of St Wilfred's. I do not say that the quality of his address was technically proficient, nor that the tone of its content was quite to my taste, but it was real. It came from the centre of him and said things that were true. I was terribly excited! I can still recall some of his comments:

In Paul's epistle to the Ephesians we read that we should put on the whole armour of God. That is, the breastplate of righteousness, the shield of faith, the helmet of salvation and the sword of the Spirit. I certainly would not presume to disagree with the great apostle, but I have to say, dear friends, that I do not find these items hanging in my spiritual wardrobe at present. I wish that they *were* there. I pray that they *will* be there. I look forward to being effective. Today, though, in my wardrobe, I find the Y-fronts of weariness, the knickers of non-involvement, the long-johns of lust, the drain-pipe trousers of drunkenness and the balaclava of bewilderment. I wear all these items at the same time and feel utterly wretched and ridiculous, but I am now looking very seriously for a change of style . . .

He also commented specifically on his own preaching style.

I am well aware [he announced] that my sermons have tended to be either boring exposition or inflated testimony. I have now decided, however, that boring expositions are boring, and that an inflated testimony sounds like some awful illness. I intend to have my inflated testimony drained at the earliest possible opportunity. Whatever remains will presumably be the truth, a truth which some of you may find very disappointing, as, no doubt, shall I. I intend, my fellow rat-bags, to invite Jesus to take the stale loaves and shrivelled little fishes of my life and distribute them to you lot Sunday by Sunday, leaving enough over each time, I trust, for me to take some home for lunch. In answer to your unspoken questions, I am not anxious to remove the pews by tomorrow morning and have a dance-floor laid down, nor have I invited Graham Kendrick into my life. I would simply like to be more honest and more useful . . .

He concluded his extraordinary address with the following words:

May I finish by saying that I am a coward. I am a coward in many areas, but particularly when it comes to sharing my scraps of faith with others. Let us pray for the courage to be generous with our poverty. As a church we are looking far too untenanted. The words of the old children's rhyme have changed significantly.

He held up his hands with the fingers linked together.

Here's the church, and here's the steeple, open the doors and here's a bit of a problem really. Pray for courage to face the problem. Amen.

I was not able to remain after the service for coffee, but I sensed that the response of the congregation was by no means uniform. The Vicar's comments and observations landed like a sudden shower of rain on those present, leaving some refreshed, some gasping for breath, and some angry at being so unexpectedly immersed in what I certainly regarded as living water.

2

I have been asked to write an account of the group meeting on the Thursday following that sermon, and I am particularly glad to do so because, like dear Hartley on the previous week, I quite deliberately arrived at the church at a much earlier time than was usual, in order to speak privately to Nunc.

How I loved Nunc! Though I knew him for only a few short weeks he became a dear friend, a valued adviser, and also (Vincent and I were not fortunate enough to have children of our own) a child who seemed to have a genuine need of the care and love that was inadequately offered to him by the small group of us who were privileged to be in close contact with him. As to the strangeness of his appearance and origins, all I can say is that after only one meeting with him, it was as though I had always known Nunc.

I entered the church through the front door on that evening at precisely six-fifteen, and at first was unable to find any trace of Nunc. After searching the body of the church itself with no success I took the key to the abutting hall from its hook in the fuse-box and unlocked the connecting door. Nunc was sitting alone at one of the square folding tables that are used for coffee and biscuits after the services and the mid-week meeting. He appeared to be speaking earnestly to an invisible companion on the opposite side of the table. I waited quietly.

'How do we do?' Nunc was saying. 'My name is not Nunc and I have never erred or strayed from his ways. I am a sheep who has never been mislaid. I am not an alien, by the way. Who is the Reverend Persimmon or Dot or Richard or Hartley? I do not know them. Nigel Forsyth is a good man who has cast the continual dew of his blessing on the Vicar, whom I do not know. I do not like him either. Most of all I do not like Dot and Hartley. They are not special to me. I do not want to see them now. I do not want to know how you are. I do not want to go home . . .'

Nunc stopped speaking. Two huge tears inflated slowly in his eyes like shining bubbles being blown up from inside his head, then they burst with a 'POP!' and ran slowly down his cheeks.

'Oh, Dot!' he said when he turned to face me, 'I was trying to find out how it feels to be a human person, but when home came out of my mouth I wished I had not opened my lips. I need to be loved, Dot.'

Nunc held out his arms towards me like a small child who has grazed his knee, touchingly confident in the warmth of my response. For one dreadful moment I came very close to failing him. I had rather feared and avoided physical expressions of affection since Vincent's death, perhaps because I suspected that it might trigger an outpouring of grief that was, if I am honest, very much overdue. I am committed to the truth, and I must therefore admit that there was also a strong element of resentment in my immediate inner response. I had arrived at St Wilfred's early with the intention of confiding in Nunc. I was in need of comfort, but now I was being asked to comfort another. It felt unfair.

Fortunately, I was able to resist these unworthy impulses (I have always believed that obedience is the gateway to love), and I do so thank God that I did. When I bent down to embrace Nunc and he buried his face in my shoulder, an extraordinary thing happened.

I found myself in the graveyard of a small Sussex church that Vincent and I had very much enjoyed visiting, during our annual holidays at a small hotel just to the north of Eastbourne. Now, however, I was walking along a narrow gravel path that curled around the west wall of this friendly little place of worship that had become such a warm holiday habit. Everything was exactly as I recalled until I passed the ancient yew tree whose berries were, as dear Vincent never tired of informing me, 'deadly poisonous'. At the foot of the gnarled old trunk stood a gravestone that had certainly not been there on previous occasions; indeed, it was not a position in which one would attempt to dig a grave under normal circumstances.

Although the day was fresh and sunny, the darkness beneath the overhanging branches of the old tree was so profound that I was unable, at first, to make out the inscription on the stone before me. Taking a few paces forward I dropped onto one knee and looked closely at the words chiselled into the black, shining surface:

VINCENT HAROLD JENKINS
BORN 16th APRIL 1910
DIED 5th AUGUST 1988
HE IS ELSEWHERE

As I read these words a sense of overwhelming sadness and

desolation shadowed my heart, and leaving the terrible message behind, I regained the path and continued to walk around the angle of the building. Just to my right now appeared the sight that Vincent and I had always looked forward to so much in our rather childlike way. The south side of the church was surrounded by bushes and tall trees in such profusion that, at this point on the path, one almost felt as if one was walking through a gloomy tunnel. But in the thick greenery that constituted one wall of the tunnel an archway had been cut to allow the presence of a low wooden stile for the passage of walkers. On the other side of the archway lay the most beautiful field, full of leggy buttercups, and sloping gently away to a sleepy river at the foot of the valley. Vincent and I always said that this shining, jewel-like vision of blue sky, green grass and golden buttercups, set like a magic-lantern slide against the dark leafy background, was a little glimpse of heaven.

Sadly, I negotiated the stile as I had done on so many occasions, except that now there was no arm to lean on as I stepped down, and no one with whom to share such a perfect day. I took a few steps forward in the long grass and stopped as the bottom of the valley came into view. Quite a large crowd of people had gathered on the riverbank, picnicking lazily in the warm sunshine or dozing at full length among the buttercups. I felt more alienated and lonely than ever at the sight of those happy folk enjoying each other's company less than a hundred yards from where I stood.

About to turn away, my attention was arrested suddenly by one man in particular. He was sitting with his back towards me, at the foot of an oak tree whose shade Vincent and I had frequently enjoyed. Something about the shape of his shoulders and the tilt of his head reminded me so strongly of Vincent that I lingered for a moment, playing in my mind with the fantasy that soon the man would turn his head and smile and wave and call out, 'Dotty darling!' just as Vincent might have done. Then the man glanced to one side so that his profile was visible to me, and my heart seemed to stop. It *was* Vincent! It *must* be Vincent! You cannot live with a man for fifty years and forget the shape of his face. I was completely unable to move.

'Vincent,' I whispered, so quietly that he could not possibly have heard me, 'Vincent, it's me – Dotty.'

As though he had heard me perfectly clearly, the man turned, full-face, and looked directly at me. All doubt disappeared. It was Vincent – fit and healthy and more relaxed than I had ever seen him. He showed no surprise whatsoever at seeing me. He simply smiled and nodded as if my arrival was exactly what he had expected, then, with a friendly wave of the hand, he turned away again, resting his wrists on his knees, and gazed out across the valley. Holding out both of my arms I took one pace towards the seated figure and found myself back in the church hall of St Wilfred's, cuddling an alien and feeling rather confused.

3

'Have you been somewhere, Dotty?' enquired Nunc, sniffing a little as I disengaged from our cuddle and took the seat that his imaginary companion had occupied on the opposite side of the table.

'Why do you call me Dotty, Nunc?' I passed him a tissue from my handbag. 'Nobody has ever called me Dotty, except . . .'

'Except?'

His eyes were wide with innocent interest.

'Except Vincent, my husband. I arrived early this evening, Nunc, because I very much wanted to share with you a great concern of mine. I am of a generation that does not easily speak about personal matters, but I do believe we are called upon to share our burdens, and I – well, I felt that you might be able to help in some way. Just now, though, when I err . . .'

'When you went somewhere?'

'Yes, when I went somewhere, I think I was granted an answer to the question that has troubled me, but I must confess that I am bewildered by that answer. You see, I am a born-again Christian, but – '

'Is there some other kind of Christian, Dot?' asked Nunc.

'I beg your pardon?'

'Perhaps I am mistaken,' said Nunc, 'but I understand from the words of your founder that the Kingdom of God is available *only* to those who have been born again. Is that not so?'

'Well, yes, you are absolutely right, of course, but nowadays the term has acquired connotations of wild-eyed, single-issue fanaticism, and one is almost embarrassed to be described in that way. However, that is what I am and I thank God for it. It was very costly . . . for him. I became a Christian in 1935, the year of my marriage, during a mission at our local church. I was, quite simply, bowed down with grief by an awareness of my sin, and subsequently deliriously joyful to learn that I was forgiven and redeemed by the blood of Jesus. An unfashionably orthodox experience, I fear, but a very genuine and lasting one. Vincent always assured me that he had experienced a similar conversion, but, as he put it, in a much quieter way. Over the years, though . . .'

'You doubted it.'

'I doubted it.'

It was the first time I had expressed my doubt to anyone at all, let alone an alien. I took a photograph from my bag and placed it on the table in front of Nunc. I was aware that my voice shook slightly as I spoke.

'Vincent was a very good man, Nunc, very strict with himself, and very highly principled. As a boy he was taught that if you do as you are told and respect authority you will be looked after. Hard work brings results, honesty is the best policy, real men don't cry, God helps those who help themselves – he lined his principles up like soldiers at a very early stage in life, and only ever reviewed them as a General reviews his troops. There was never any question of change or flexibility. He was generous to me, and to others whom he loved or respected, but he had little or no tolerance for law-breakers or vagrants or limp failures. You became what you were through effort or lack of effort and that's all there was to it.'

'Was he really like that?' asked Nunc.

'I know that there was a troubled little boy inside my husband, Nunc. Once, when he was only six years old, there was a family break-up of some kind. Vincent was sent away to a house in the country to be looked after by people he had never seen before. He had no idea why he had gone, how long he would be there or when he would next see a familiar face. Like the little soldier he had been taught to be, he never cried once for the whole of the eleven months that he spent in that place. Then he went home.'

I picked up the photograph and studied it as I spoke.

'I don't think the – perplexity of that year away from home ever left Vincent. It created a tenderness that very few people saw. I saw it – I loved it. He *was* a good man, but . . .'

'But he was not a Christian?'

I placed the photograph carefully back in my handbag.

'I have always worried that he was not. It added greatly to my grief on his death three years ago from cancer. That is why I was surprised just now by my own conviction that Vincent is – safe, and that I shall see him again. Thrilled, of course, but surprised.'

We sat in silence for more than a minute. Somewhere in the distance a door opened and closed. Hartley mentioned in his account of the previous week's meeting the peculiar way in which Nunc glowed at certain times. Hartley makes the quite reasonable assumption that this occurred at those times when Nunc was praying, and that assumption may well be a correct one, although I never heard Nunc himself account for it in that way. Be that as it may, it began to happen now, and he was still illuminated when the Vicar came crashing through the connecting door from the church.

'There you are!' he said loudly, 'trying to hide from me, eh?'

He dragged a chair across the floor and settled himself at the table with a great deal of scraping and shuffling and puffing and blowing. I am very fond of David Persimmon, but he is not a man who is sensitive to atmosphere.

'You know, Nunc,' he said, 'if you ever get tired of being an alien you could always earn a crust by hiring yourself out as a peripatetic table lamp. What are we talking about?'

'David,' I said, 'please could we not be flippant for a moment? Something happened just now – perhaps I shall be able to describe it to you on another occasion – and it suggested to me that Vincent has found – that he is safe with Jesus. I have been telling Nunc that my joy is mingled with puzzlement. I know that God is always merciful and quick to meet us if we approach him, but I honestly did not believe that Vincent had ever genuinely made this approach, or understood God's love for him.'

'So he ought to be down in the other place, eh?'

'David, I cannot *make* my Bible say the things that I would like it to say.'

'Really? Most people can, Dot. You'd better not let old Craven hear this particular piece of theology. He makes your average universalist look like Calvin's godson. Actually, Dot . . .'

The Vicar began to tap the table furiously and rhythmically with the end of one finger, kneading his face with the other hand as though attempting to remodel his features. I waited. Finally, he placed both hands flat on the table, stared at them for a moment, then spoke.

'Dot, something did happen to Vincent.' He paused. 'I spent quite a lot of time with your old man during those last few months, as you know. Got quite fond of the stubborn old whatnot.'

I smiled reminiscently. Vincent had loved David. He made him laugh and was never sentimental or tragic. But this was the first I had heard of something 'happening'. I felt quite nervous.

'I'm going to tell you something now, Dot, that Vincent asked me to keep to myself. No, don't worry – he didn't have shares in the white-slave trade. It was something that happened to him after his second operation. As I said, he asked me to keep it to myself, but I think – ' I noticed that he glanced at Nunc, who was no longer glowing ' – I think he'd like me to tell you now, so I'm going to.

'Vincent had that second op on the Thursday night, and I saw him in the ward the following day. They hadn't let you see him by then, but for some insane reason they think patients don't mind being persecuted by the clergy, so they let me in. Vincent was in bed about halfway down the ward – remember? – and he didn't look too bad considering what he'd been through. But I'd only just got started on his grapes and settled on his commode when the poor old chap burst into tears. Woomph! Just like that.

'When he'd calmed down a bit he told me he'd had a sort of "experience" that he wanted to tell me about, but when he tried to describe it he kept getting so choked up that it took quite a long time to get it all out. Leaving out the chokes, this is what happened.

'Old Vince came out of the killing jar that night feeling sore, exhausted, angry and frightened. Just to make things worse, they'd shipped a new patient into the bed immediately opposite Vince's and he really was in a dreadful state. Vince reckoned he must have been brought in off the streets, because he was absolutely filthy, covered in sores and scabs and other unspeakable things. He was naked and completely exposed after kicking his sheets onto the floor, and, just to complete the picture, he screamed and swore and shouted abuse without stopping. In short – a real charmer.

'Vince said he'd never ever felt so homicidal. Having someone like that opposite him at that particular time was almost too much to bear. Far from feeling Christian sympathy for his fellow patient, Vincent said that if he'd had the strength to cross the ward he would have put the man out of his misery – one smart blow with a bed-pan would probably have done it. Besides, this was just the sort of chap, if you don't mind me saying so, Dot, that Vince couldn't stick at any price. A no-hoper, a parasite, a useless member of society, probably alcoholic, a waste of time. He despised and hated him.

'Well, that night, staff were a bit thin on the ground in Vincent's ward, and it was some time before the Sister in charge got round to dealing with the new patient. She was a big girl, this nurse, and Vince watched with real relish as she drew the curtains round the man opposite. "Now he's had it!" said Vince to himself, "she'll fix him!"

'Now, as it happened, the curtains were only drawn along the sides of the wild man's bed, so Vince was able to see everything that happened in the opposite bed space. He said it was like having a little private theatre set up, just so that he could watch what was going on.

'So, in goes this muscular lady, but instead of getting angry and aggressive with the bloke, she sat down on the side of the bed, took him into her arms like a baby, and started singing to him and stroking his head and talking to him as if nothing and nobody else in the world meant as much to her as he did. And she carried on doing that until he was just lying quietly, sores, scabs and all, wrapped up in those big arms of hers. And do you know what Vincent did, Dot? He cried – he broke down and cried like a baby in his bed on the other side of the ward. He cried for the hardness of his heart, and his intolerance, and most of all – most of all he cried because in that bed space opposite he'd seen – and these were *his* words: he'd seen for the first time that God loved *him*, and that he was just as scabby inside as the man opposite was scabby outside. He was like a little boy, Dot, just like a little boy.'

'Like a little boy of six,' I whispered, as David finished speaking. 'Dear Vincent – I wonder why he never told me.'

David frowned and shook his head uncertainly.

'Difficult to say, Dot. My own guess is that he thought one brief spiritual experience didn't count for much next to your fifty-odd years of Bible-bashing, so he just tucked it away and kept it to himself. Took it with him when he went, of course, as well.'

So happy was I, that I did not even rebuke David for describing my half-century walk with Jesus as 'fifty years of Bible-bashing'. Indeed, I was so very grateful to him that I fear I embarrassed him slightly by kissing him quite warmly on the cheek. I was rescued from the inevitable flippancy of his response by a question from Nunc.

'What is Bible-bashing, Dot, and why have you been doing it for fifty years?'

'Far too complicated to answer! Blast!' cried David, as he sprang to his feet knocking over his chair in the process. 'Let's go and put the seats out.'

David can be very forceful at times.

4

'What have you been working on lately, Craven?' asked the Vicar a little later, when we were all assembled in the church. 'Let me see now, I think I can remember the titles of your last few books. *Space Warriors from Drenkel III*, that was the first one wasn't it? Then there was *It shouldn't happen to a Space Warrior from Drenkel III*, and who could forget *Let sleeping Space Warriors from Drenkel III lie*. And my particular favourite, *All Space Warriors from Drenkel III great and small*. And what's in the pipeline? Could it be *If only Space Warriors from Drenkel III could talk*? And then, I suppose we may expect – '

'May I enquire, David,' interrupted Richard with great dignity, 'whether this heavy-handed humour is yet another attempt on your part to persuade me that I should bend my literary attention towards some kind of spiritual subject?'

'Yes,' said the Vicar, 'it is, except that I wouldn't have put it so pompously.'

'David,' I interposed gently, 'have you actually read any of Richard's books?'

Richard shook his head. 'I don't believe he has, Dot.'

'Now look, Craven, I can tell you without a whisper of a lie that I have read every single word in your books – '

'Come off it! You haven't – '

'Only not in the order you wrote them, you understand . . .'

'Nor,' said Richard, 'does he know anything whatsoever about science fiction as a genre. He thinks Kurt Vonnegut Junior is a Bavarian tap-dancer, don't you, Dave?'

'I don't even know what a genre is,' replied David, looking so melancholy that I simply could not refrain from laughing.

'Dot may laugh, but it's not easy when you're made like me. I'm very disappointed in my brain. It doesn't seem able to concentrate on anything that isn't immediately captivating for more than about two minutes. And I've never been that interested in science fiction anyway. I get as far as learning that Elmed Brarg, the flange-keeper of Zim, has challenged the mighty Vorgans to galactic combat, and I just can't face any more. I'm sure it's a fault in me, but there it is.'

Richard slapped the sides of his chair in exasperation.

'That's just a ludicrous caricature, Dave,' he said. 'All this "flange-keeper of Zim" stuff is about as far removed from my books as the Pope is from some British house church leaders . . .'

Dear Hartley, who had been listening quietly with a most bewildered expression on his face, clearly thought that the time had arrived for an intelligent question.

'Mr Craven,' he said, leaning forward in his chair, 'what is the difference between the Pope and some British house church leaders?'

'Oh, they're completely different, Hartley,' answered Richard. 'The Pope is an autocrat who rules over an empire of people, many of whom are naïvely trusting in . . . yes, well, I suppose there isn't much difference when you think about it. Still – '

'You've been waiting five years for someone to ask you that question, haven't you, Dick? Admit it!' The Vicar leaned back in his chair and guffawed loudly.

'Still!' persisted Richard with a smile, 'even if I have to

find a different comparison, the fact remains that sophisticated science fiction can be as subtle and meaningful as any other kind of literature. Isaac Asimov – '

'Does 'e?' interrupted David, adding penitently, 'sorry, Dot' as I caught his eye. I cannot stand vulgarity.

'All right,' said Richard, 'never mind rational argument. It's obviously a waste of time. Look, I wasn't going to tell you this, Dave, but I *have* been doing a bit of research on something connected with the church. I didn't want to tell you because I knew you'd produce twenty-three bad jokes about me thinking I was the new C. S. Lewis. If you want me to tell you about it I will, but only if you take it seriously. Agreed?'

The Vicar opened his eyes and mouth to their full extent and gestured widely with his hands, as if imploring heaven to witness that Richard's comments were a foul slur on one so innocent.

'Do you want to hear or not?' persisted Richard, ignoring the extravagant dumb-show. 'It's quite important to me.'

At last the seriousness of Richard's manner seemed to make an impact on David. At heart he is the kindest of men.

'Of course I want to hear, Dick,' he said, 'it's me who keeps going on at you about changing direction, isn't it?'

'All right, I'll tell you.' Richard rose from his chair and paced to and fro for a few moments before speaking again. 'It's history really. I thought to myself, "What's the best way to get into this other area of writing?" And then it occurred to me that the best – the most obvious place to start would be my own church. What did I actually *know* about my own church? It's called St Wilfred's. Why? Who was this Wilfred, and what did he do that caused him to be made a saint! So that's what I started with – the search for Wilfred. And, in a way, Dave, I did it for you.'

'I *know* where Wilfred is,' announced Hartley unexpectedly, 'he is in the big window over the altar.'

'Ah, yes,' said Richard, 'that's certainly a picture of the Wilfred that we usually associate with this church, but, after a great deal of reading and research, I learned that our church is, in fact, named after a quite different Wilfred, one whose claim to fame is, as Sherlock Holmes would put it, singular in the extreme.'

The enthusiasm in Richard's voice had, by now, communicated itself strongly to David, who, with narrowed eyes and slightly tilted head, was giving the speaker his entire attention. Nunc, on the other hand, when I glanced at him, was wearing a curious little smile. Almost unconsciously I drew my chair back a little to avoid the explosion that was likely to occur very shortly.

'I discovered,' went on Richard, sitting down in his chair and radiating excited intensity, 'that Wilfred – our Wilfred – was a sort of mediaeval monk who belonged to an order of believers who were committed, not only to prayer and all the usual things, but also to the "bodily comforts and nourishment of the brethren". They used all their wealth and time and energy in supplying food and drink to any person or persons engaged in the Lord's work in the area where their houses were established. Also, of course, they had a tradition of warm hospitality towards all visitors.

'Now, they took the food side of their work remarkably seriously. People tend to believe that mediaeval food was just a sort of grey sludge, but that was not the case. Wilfred and his brothers were committed to quality in the planning, preparation and attractive presentation of the meals that they provided for others – because they were doing it for God, you see?'

David nodded mechanically, but otherwise remained quite motionless, listening like a man hypnotized.

'And Wilfred's job – his specific job – was to develop and to experiment with new puddings and sweet foods of all kinds. I know it sounds trivial nowadays, but for Wilfred it was his own special responsibility and ministry, and he gave his life to it. In the end he went off into the Sahara (his particular branch of the order was in North Africa) and settled there with a little band of brothers and novices to concentrate on the invention and testing of good, wholesome puddings. And that little group came to be known by a special name, a name that I shall use as the title of my historical work if and when I complete my study of Wilfred's life.'

'What was Wilfred's little group called?' asked the Vicar in a hushed but fascinated voice.

'They were known,' said Richard solemnly, 'as the Dessert Fathers.'

During the Second World War, when I was staying with my Aunt Myrtle in London, I experienced the terrible silence that followed the passing overhead of a flying bomb, and which immediately preceded the dreadful explosion as it landed. The silence that followed this last remark of Richard's was extraordinarily similar in quality, although when David *did* speak, it was in the same hushed tone that he had used before.

'I'm going to kill you, Craven,' he said, 'slowly,

painfully, and with the utmost enjoyment, and I'm going to do it now.'

He rose to his feet and moved slowly towards Richard, his hands extended with clutching fingers, like a strangler in a Victorian melodrama. Richard raised a restraining hand.

'Dave, before you kill me – '

The Vicar froze in his threatening posture.

'Just before you kill me,' repeated the cowering historian, 'there was one more thing about Wilfred I forgot to tell you. As a teenager he – he was something of an anoraksic . . .'

The play-fight that followed was extremely undignified, but oddly endearing. David and Richard wrestled like small boys until, inevitably, David's superior weight and strength dominated, and he ended up sitting on Richard's chest, pinning his opponent's arms down with his knees and waving a rolled-up newspaper taken from his side pocket.

'I'm going to bash you with the *Daily Mail*, Craven,' he cried, 'until you take a conservative view of our dearly beloved Wilfred, who has been turning in his stained-glass window throughout the pathetic story – '

' – that fooled you completely,' gasped Richard recklessly.

'I shall release you when you apologize to Wilfred,' pronounced the Vicar, tapping his victim smartly on the head with the end of his newspaper. 'Come on now – apologize!'

'Forgive me, Wilfred!' appealed Richard in piteous tones, adding, as he was released and allowed to stand, 'it's a good job you didn't hit me with the *News of the World*,

Persimmon – you'd have heard some juicy details about your precious Wilfred then.' He chuckled richly. 'You should've seen your face just now, Dave. Hook, line and sinker! Scores even, eh?'

'Yes, blast you, Craven!' agreed David, flopping back on his seat with exhaustion. '"Experiment with new puddings . . ."! How could I be taken in by such drivel? Perhaps I ought to read your stuff after all, Dick, if it's all as convincing as that.'

'Dot, may I ask you something please?'

Nunc was always *so* polite and charming.

'Of course, dear,' I replied, 'ask whatever you wish.'

'Why have you been hitting your Bible with the *Daily Mail* for fifty strange years?'

I could see David mentally wrestling with the complexity of this misunderstanding, but I saw immediately how Nunc had arrived at his – apparently – nonsensical question.

'David should have answered your earlier question when it was asked, Nunc,' I said. 'When he spoke of my "Bible-bashing" he meant – at least I hope he meant – my affinity with, and love for the word of God. And "fifty-odd years" simply means a number of years between fifty and sixty.'

'Oh,' said Nunc, 'I see.'

'But let me ask *you* a question, Nunc. What did you think of Richard's story about St Wilfred? Did you believe what he said?'

'Oh, no!' Nunc's eyes shone. 'I knew it was a game. Wilfred would be most amused to be described as a maker of puddings . . .'

It was entirely typical of our contact with Nunc, that

no one asked him how he knew that Wilfred would be 'most amused'. Not least because, after comments of the latter kind, Nunc's face would drop like that of a child who has unintentionally given away a secret, and he would look from one to another in our little group, almost as though he was pleading silently with us to not notice what he had said. At such times, the very air inside the ancient stone building seemed somehow to shiver with secrets so deep and yet so close, that we were all too happy to move quickly on to some other subject.

5

'I believed Mr Craven,' said Hartley. 'I liked the story.'

'It was a very good story, Hartley,' agreed David, 'but the whole idea of it was to change the subject. The very aptly named Mr Craven avoids the subject of writing something useful in the same way that a frightened child runs past a graveyard.'

I felt that I could not let this pass.

'I am not a science fiction fan myself, David, but unlike you I have read one of Richard's books. It was original, ingenious and extremely well written. Thousands of people find a great deal of enjoyment in his work. It seems to me that your assumption that a book is not useful unless it is specifically Christian in content is rather arrogant.

'At least he's consistent,' muttered Richard.

'I'm not saying that at all, Dot. I know as well as you do that the bulk of so-called Christian literature could put Andrex out of business if it wasn't being used to build supporting walls in Christian book shops. I just think that

Dick has got the style and the approach to give us something we really need.'

Richard did not look flattered. In fact (as Hartley so well expressed it in his own account) his face had taken on a cold, locked-up expression.

'And this carefully considered view,' he said, 'has been reached despite the fact that you've never taken the trouble to read anything that I've written? You really are remarkable Reverend Persimmon.'

'I don't need to read anything you've written,' replied David simply. 'I've heard you speak and I just know. Besides,' he went on, recrossing his legs as he warmed to his theme, 'you can still use your science fiction. Surely you could put a lot of truth across using fantasy. Other people have.'

'Oh yes, of course they have, haven't they? Particularly in the area of fiction for children, unless I'm very much mistaken.' Richard's voice contained an ugly, sneering note. 'You may be surprised to hear that I've read a great deal of it – enough to last me a good long time, that's for sure.'

'There is some fine literature for children, Richard,' I asserted gently, 'do you not agree?'

'It seems to me,' said Richard, in the same mocking voice, 'that modern Christian children must have a very confused picture of the spiritual life. In all these books they read about ordinary children having wonderful adventures in strange worlds. To get into these other worlds they go through the backs of wardrobes – '

'A wonderful story!' I could not help but exclaim.

'One of my favourite books,' added Hartley.

'To get into these other worlds,' repeated Richard,

slicing coldly through the warmth of our response, 'they go through the backs of wardrobes, down hollow oak trees, into pictures that are hanging on the living room wall; they ride off on magic bicycles or go on neatly metaphorical journeys, just about anything *but* normal activities. And they have the most wonderful adventures designed to show the reader that – guess what? – the Christian life is also a wonderful adventure.'

'Why is that wrong?' asked David.

'Because it's not a wonderful adventure.' Richard's voice was suddenly full of passion. 'It's nothing to do with how good the books are. What I'm saying is that it's not fair to let children believe that some great Raiders of the Lost Ark-type adventure is waiting for them just round the corner, when, in fact, they're likely to be, at best, bored by God, and, at worst, let down by him just when they need him most. There's nothing more disappointing for children than to find out that the grown-ups have lied to them – again!'

I think we were all rather stunned for a moment. There was such an intense hurt behind Richard's words that one hesitated to disagree with him. Nevertheless, I knew that I must speak.

'Richard, dear,' I said, as quietly and kindly as I could, 'I have to say to you that the last half-century really and truly and honestly has been the most marvellously exciting adventure with Jesus, as far as I am concerned.'

Richard looked straight into my eyes as he spoke again.

'Dot, I believe what you say because I've never known you to tell anything but the truth. But your experience is not the same as mine, and if your God is also my God, then I don't understand what's going on. Do you know how it seems to me sometimes? I feel as if I've been left behind by God. But before he went he gave me a coin. "Keep tossing the coin," he said, "and as soon as you throw 'heads' twenty times consecutively I'll come back and get you, and everything will be all right. Don't worry – although you won't be able to see me, I'll be here with you when you toss the coin, influencing the way it falls – as long as you remain faithful."

'For a long time I believed what he'd said. Over and over again I would send that coin up into the air, rejoicing gratefully whenever it came up heads, and examining my attitude and conduct with penitent concern when it landed on tails. Sometimes, to my great excitement, I would throw nine, or even ten heads in a row. When that happened I *knew* that God was with me, and that, one day, I would achieve my twenty consecutive heads, and be with him forever. When I threw the same number of tails I felt that I must have committed an unforgivable sin or embraced some numismatical heresy; or I might accept the word of an established expert that the throwing of ten tails was a necessary "dark night of the soul": or perhaps even that my faith in the managing director of the mint was being tested.

'How I argued with those who said my faith was misplaced! How I stretched and distorted my fiscal theology to accommodate disappointments. How I subdued my own fear that I was battling against a statistical impossibility by telling myself, again and again, that with God involved anything was possible. And then it started . . .'

Richard rose to his feet and slowly crossed the church until he was standing beneath a picture on the north wall, showing Mary at the foot of the cross. After studying it for a few seconds, he turned and came back towards us, stopping just outside the circle of chairs and staring into the distance as he spoke.

'It became more and more difficult to convince myself that the way heads and tails were coming up was anything but random – just a normal, predictable distribution. I'd tried so hard to make it all true, but it wasn't. I was never going to throw my twenty heads, and he wasn't going to come back, and I wasn't going to be with him for ever, and I didn't want to be with him anyway because I hated him. Nasty, narrow little God who lets a few in and shuts the others out and tells lies to people who trust him.'

'Now that's entrails for you!' said David, most insensitively and unwisely in my view. Richard turned on him with a quite heart-rending mixture of entreaty and fury.

'What's the matter with you?' he shouted. 'I thought, judging by your sermon on Sunday, that you'd been born again – yet again. You were going to invite Jesus to do something or other, weren't you? Do you think there's any chance of him making you take your friends seriously when they let out a bit of their pain for the first time in God knows how long? Or will most of the divine energy go into getting your smile right? Two or three more sermons like that and you'll be on the old conference circuit, Dave, with a clean neck like Nick and Sue, and a lot of very real compassion for lost souls like me. Well, hallelujah up yours, mate!'

David actually turned pale. 'We've always joked,' he said, 'even when we're serious – we've joked.' He went on in a low voice. 'Something happened to me last week. You

know it did – you were here. It didn't turn me into Billy
Graham or anything like that. I just saw that I'd probably
been blaming the wrong people. You were pleased at the
time. You *seemed* pleased. I haven't changed really; I just
want to clear away some of the garbage and start again. Do
I have to apologize to you for that, Dick?'

'You've always been the same deep down, haven't you?'
Richard was still furious. 'You've always belonged to
Jesus down in your boots! All the blustering and the jokes
and the "God's on holiday" stuff – it's all been a way of
filling in time until the gospel train arrives at Persimmon
Halt to take you off to Glory. Something happened to you
last week. Congratulations! It's been tails every time for
me for a very long time!'

Richard moved to the foot of the steps and stood with
his back to us, his shoulders rising and falling as he sought
to control his feelings with deep, shuddering breaths.

'Richard, I don't really understand, dear.' I paused,
searching for the correct words. 'David's sermon on
Sunday was wonderfully refreshing. It had hope and
reality in it – things that this church needs, things that we
all need. I don't understand why you should be so angry
because David belongs to Jesus, as you put it. How can
that hurt you? *Why* will it hurt you?'

Richard dropped to the steps as if his power to stand had
been abruptly switched off, all his anger dissolving in
grief, like a child who finally gives up his bad behaviour
and admits to unhappiness.

'Because I shall be on my own,' he said brokenly,
'because the only other person who didn't mind being
with me where I was, is going away to *do it*! We've always
laughed and commented and poked fun at the people who

are *doing it*! Now he's going to go and *be* one! He's going to end up strong and sure and balanced and Christian and far, far away, and I – I can't . . .'

David's eyes were wild, and I had not the faintest idea what to do or say, so it was just as well that Hartley's good sense took over. He moved through the soft white light without fuss, sat down on the steps and put his arm around the shoulders of the bowed figure beside him. When Hartley looked up and spoke, it was not to David or me, but to Nunc.

'I think that Mr Craven was cross with God because of Edna,' he said quietly.

David looked up, puzzled. He and Richard had become very close friends since his arrival in the parish, but obviously not close enough for Richard to talk about the younger sister who had shared his bachelor home until her death some ten or eleven years previously.

'Edna?' said David, 'who's Edna?'

Richard raised a tear-stained face from his cupped hands.

'Edna was my sister,' he said weakly, 'she lived with me until she died in nineteen seventy-nine. She was sick for ages. The last five years of her life were an endless round of hospitals, tablets, pain-clinics and all the other ghastly paraphernalia that goes with chronic terminal illness.'

'I knew her, didn't I, Mr Craven?'

'You did, Hartley,' said Richard, patting the hand that lay on his shoulder. 'She was all right, old Edna, wasn't she, mate?'

'I played board games with her,' said Hartley, 'and she went white when her stomach hurt, and said that she would be fine in no time. She thanked God for everything,

and said that Richard was a dear old idiot who would have
to be let in the back door of heaven because he would be
too proud to come in the front. And she was always writing
to people who wrote to her, telling them that everything
would sort itself out in the end. And her favourite writer of
books was Jane Austen, and her favourite person was
Jesus – the same as Dot – and she wanted to marry Robert
Redford or Paul Newman and when she laughed you
couldn't help laughing as well, and just before she went to
hospital the last time she gave me a piece of paper and said,
"Pray this for Richard, Hartley, darling", and when I
looked at it, it said, "Lord, let his need overtake his
stubbornness one day", and I have prayed it most days
ever since, although I do not understand it. And I miss
her very much.'

'You're wonderful, Hartley,' said Richard, smiling
bleakly. 'I couldn't have described her better myself. "Let
his need overtake his stubbornness" eh? Crafty old Edna –
still praying for me twelve years after she's gone. That's
quite something. And Hartley's absolutely right, Nunc, I
am cross with God because of Edna – very cross.

'It wasn't just God though, you see, it was God's people
as well – or some of them. "Had Edna stepped outside the
Lord's will?" our more evangelical brethren enquired.
"Didn't we realize," others wanted to know, "that prayers
can be answered with 'Yes', 'No', or 'Wait'?"'

'Makes God sound like Graham Gooch,' muttered
David.

'When she was at her worst – and it was a very bad worst
– some people would cross the road rather than talk to me;
and in the very last days, when I took her out in the chair –
when she was nearly bald and her flesh was pretty well

transparent, we'd meet folk who said, "Oh, Edna, you're looking so well, so much better than when we last saw you," but she wasn't. Edna said we mustn't be hard on them because they were basically well meaning and didn't really understand, but I wasn't saintly like her, so I just hated them.'

'And the nasty little god that you spoke of?' queried Nunc.

That stopped Richard in his tracks for a moment. He looked at Nunc as though a new thought had momentarily obstructed his flow of emotion, then he set his jaw and continued grimly.

'God,' he said, 'decided that it would be appropriate for my sister to suffer unspeakable agony repeatedly, despite the fact that she talked to him, read about him, defended him and recommended him to anyone who would listen. She never blamed him once for what was happening to her, even after nights when she screamed to him to have mercy on her and he didn't. "I trust him," she would say, and I'd grit my teeth and say nothing for her sake, but inside I ached to confront him and ask him *why* she had to go through all that, so that when he gave me some twee little theological answer I could punch him on the nose, and say "That's for Edna, who kept hoping you would say 'Yes' instead of 'No' and 'Wait', and was disappointed in the end."'

'*Was* she disappointed in the end?' asked Nunc.

'No, damn it, she wasn't! I was and she wasn't. The night before she died she said, "Richard, I have the most extraordinary feeling that I shall be quite well in the morning." I went through to her at six-thirty the next day and she looked just as frail and ill as she had done the night before, but there was a sort of excitement in her – like a child who's looking forward to a treat. I asked her if she wanted me to read a passage from her Bible as usual, but she said I could put it away because she wouldn't be needing it any more, and then she asked me to put my arms round her for a little while . . .'

My own personal grief had risen so near to the surface as a result of Richard's account that I was barely able to contain it as he continued in slow, almost trance-like tones.

'And then, it was really very strange, she opened her eyes very wide and turned her head on the pillow as if she'd heard something. A great light came into her eyes, and I have to admit that for one infinitesimal moment, she looked as well as she'd ever done, and she said, "Richard, someone's calling me by name!" Then she closed her eyes and never opened them again, and I was on my own.'

I am not a spontaneous person, and I suspect that if I had allowed myself the briefest pause for reflection I would have remained in my seat. As it was, I simply surrendered to an impulse to join Richard and Hartley on the steps. The words I spoke seemed entirely relevant at the time.

'I miss Vincent so much!'

Richard, Hartley and I were, if you will excuse the ill-chosen mixture of metaphors, a huddle of bursting dams, and, I am bound to say, I believe that this outpouring of emotion did us a great deal of good. By the time we were all recovered and tissues had been distributed, David had quite uncharacteristically prepared a tray of drinks, and we sipped appreciatively for a minute or two before David, who was still rather pale, looked up over the mug he was cuddling like a hand-warmer and nodded in Richard's direction.

'The first time I encountered this bloke,' he said, 'was at a family service soon after I came here. As you might have noticed, children's work is not exactly my strong suit. Uncle Davy doesn't really know what to say to the kiddiewinks – in fact, I turn into Basil Fawlty after a few minutes, and threaten them with hanging or flogging if they don't start enjoying and appreciating my carefully prepared material. Anyway, on this particular occasion I told them an instructive little story which they didn't understand in the slightest, and then I moved on to a little quiz that I'd prepared (Christians can have fun as well as being serious, you know). With my top lip stuck to my teeth and dear Nigel Forsyth (whom I love with every fibre of my being since being totally metamorphosed last week) looking pityingly at me from the front row, I launched into a series of questions that could have been answered by a deaf, dumb, blind pagan who's been in solitary confinement all his life. They had to be easy questions in order to raise my stock with the doting parents who operate their children's arms from behind like puppeteers. "Name someone we pray to whose name begins with G," that was one of them, and "What do you call the place you come to every Sunday with your family?" One little girl thought the answer to that one might be "Grandma's house", but the rest of 'em seemed to agree that it could be "church".

'Then I came to about the third or fourth question: "Name one of the main characters in Genesis."

'"Phil Collins," said a man's voice from the cheap seats at the back.

'"What great event is Moses famous for?" I asked a bit

later on.

' "Four hundred metres hurdles," drawled the same voice.

'Some people laughed and some people didn't. Nigel Forsyth waited to see if I was embarrassed. If I had been he would have opted to join the laughers, but I wasn't – I was very amused, so he looked deeply concerned and disapproving. Afterwards, at the church door, when I was accepting the many warm compliments that my superb sermon had attracted, I spotted the comedian from the back row and decided to have a little chat with him. Do you remember that, Dick?'

Richard nodded, the old familiar smile on his face. Clearly, it was a pleasant memory.

'Every word,' he avowed. 'You said, "I think you probably need some heavy shepherding, mate," and I said, "I think I'll wait till Cyril Smith gets ordained." Then General and Mrs Ashby-Vaughn squashed between us, looking and sounding like angry walruses, and barked at you about preaching on the parables instead of the sacraments, and after they'd rumbled off I said, "Last of the dinosaurs," and you said, "Yes, big teeth, but no future." Have I got it right?'

'Word perfect, Dick,' said the Vicar, 'and over the next few weeks we became friends, until, as far as I was concerned – I'm only likely to ever say this once, so you'd better listen carefully, Craven – as far as I was concerned, and am *still* concerned, you are one of the very few people (most of the others are here tonight) who've made life bearable in this benighted parish. You make me laugh. You make me think. You don't condemn me. You don't minister to me. You're going to poison Nigel Forsyth for me on Wednesday evening. You're my friend, Dick, and I love you. Just because my budgies have become hatched-again doesn't mean our friendship is going to change. I need you more than ever, to stop me wafting away up seductively luminous dead-end tunnels. So don't get crabby, mate. I'm still here – honestly . . .'

Richard drew in one big breath, held it for a moment, then seemed to dispel it and his resistance to David's warmth at the same time.

'I'm a bit of a headless chicken tonight, Dave.' He sat upright and looked round at us all. 'I can't believe this is me. I just don't do this – this entrails stuff. I'm glad it happened here, but I'm confused, very confused.'

'How many people have left you behind, Richard?' asked Nunc quietly.

'I expect you're right really,' said Richard, answering Nunc's meaning rather than his question. 'Makes quite a list when I think about it. Father died when I was a toddler, Mum left me with Edna when I was just about to go off to university, couple of obligatory failed love affairs, then Edna. And . . . in a general sort of way, I suppose I think God's cleared off as well.'

Nunc nodded solemnly. 'It is meet and right that he should clear off.'

'You mean it's a good idea?' Richard looked rather surprised.

'Oh yes,' said Nunc, 'I would not like to meet the nasty narrow little God who played that silly game with you about doing things twenty times in a row. I do not think he exists. I think you have made him. But if he did exist I would not want to know him. I would hate him as much as you do. I do not think you have really been angry with

God. You have been angry with people for leaving you alone, especially Edna. You must forgive her. You must meet her God.'

'The one who let her suffer?'

'The one she loved and trusted even though she was suffering. The one who called her by name. I have found a book of songs in this Church of England that sometimes makes me think of him. He is not a God who does not care, he is a hurting God who cares more for Edna than you do. The song that reminds me most of him has these words in it:

I cannot tell how silently he suffered,
As with his peace he graced this place of tears,
Or how his heart upon the cross was broken,
The crown of pain to three-and-thirty years.
But this I know, he heals the broken-hearted,
And stays our sin, and calms our lurking fear,
And lifts the burden from the heavy laden,
For yet the Saviour, Saviour of the world, is here.

He is not a nasty, narrow little God, Richard. Edna loved him and now they are together. Why did you continue to come to church after she died?'

It was an abrupt question, but Richard answered without a pause.

'To be near her, and . . .'

'And?'

'Twenty or thirty years ago I thought I met the God you've been talking about – all tambourines and Bible-notes I was for a little while, and then, what with one thing and another, he didn't seem to come up with the goods and it all faded. I suppose, sitting here week after week, I thought – if that God, Edna's God, was all she cracked him up to be, he might . . . well, do something. That's why, when Martin Luther here became a sunbeam – joking, Dave – I felt hurt and angry; with Dave because he seemed to be going for early rapture on his own, and with God because he hadn't done something to change *me*. I've been waiting for years to experience a tiny bit of what Edna did. I know it's childish, but it just doesn't seem fair.'

'What about all that stuff last week about the people who know you best being aware that you're a closet charismatic?' asked David.

Richard shook his head sadly. 'The nearest I've come to ecstatic utterance was when Arsenal won the league. I said it to keep you all off my back. Didn't work, did it?'

'Speak to Edna's God, Richard,' said Nunc, with an authority that seemed quite unconnected to the sad, childlike little person whom I had comforted earlier in the evening. 'When you are at home, speak to Edna's God. Acknowledge all your transgressions. He will run to meet you. Speak to him.'

'If I speak to him,' whispered Richard, his eyes unnaturally bright, 'will he speak to me?'

'He will speak to you now,' said Nunc, 'about the sadness you have known.'

Of all the strange things that happened during the period that Nunc was among us, the next thing that occurred on that evening was, for me, the most beautiful of all. Nunc slipped off his chair, held out his hand to take Richard's and led him right up to the big stone altar, where the two of them knelt between the giant grey candle-sticks that stood on either side. Suddenly the two

candles were alight, and all other illumination had disappeared. I remember how struck I was by the contrast between the child's silhouette on one side and the slightly broken shape of the man on the other.

As they knelt together, a song filled the church. It was a single voice, unaccompanied by instruments of any kind, and if you ask me to describe it, I can only say that it was the most perfect, pure, choir-boy's voice that I have ever heard, and that the tune of the song was simple and unadorned, but, at the same time, indescribably moving. I shall not forget the words that rang through St Wilfred's that evening, if I live to be a thousand years old. Nor will I forget the quite inexplicable sense in which sadness and sympathy seemed to settle on Richard like the very gentlest summer rain.

> Evensong, twilight tune
> Sad goodbyes, see you soon
> Every night seems so long
> I want to hear your evensong.
>
> Autumn days, ice-cream air
> Summer's gone, a failed prayer
> Lines of grey in auburn hair
> Faded pictures, leave them there.
>
> Seaside town, winter's day
> Empty streets, cold and grey
> Waves of comfort blown to spray
> Who will hear me when I pray?

All my life, waiting for
Knowing you, being sure
Tiny glimpses through the door
Shining moments shine no more.

Evensong, twilight tune
Sad goodbyes, see you soon
Every night seems so long
I want to hear your evensong.

When Nunc and Richard returned we stood as a group with our arms around each other, and David said gently, 'I don't think I'm the only one who doesn't mind being with you where you are, Dick,' then he threw his arms wide and spoke in a loud and unusually confident way. 'We are the body of Christ! We, the lost and the found, the sure and the unsure, the joyful and the sad, the native and the alien, the wise and the simple, the Vicar and the organist, the healthy and the sick, those who depart and those who return, those in the light and those in darkness, those who are saintly and those who are not – all who say yes to the suffering, triumphant Jesus – we are the body of Christ, and we need you!'

And as we all said 'Amen!' the light shone from Nunc, who was beside me facing David, so that a huge shadow was thrown onto the west wall of the church, and the shape of the shadow was like nothing so much as a giant cross, and I suddenly longed for heaven.

Part Four

Richard's Account

Richard's Account

1

Some years ago I took a taxi from Victoria Station to Liverpool Street on my way to a book evening in the beautiful city of Norwich. The chap who drove my taxi was an older man, with what I always imagine to be a cockney accent, and a very pleasant, courteous manner. I enjoy travelling in London taxis – they would make a wonderful fairground ride.

On this occasion, just before reaching our objective, we were overtaken and forced over by a red, open-topped sports car, driven by a young man with Biggles-style neck-scarf, dark glasses and shining, brushed-back hair. My driver said nothing at the time, but a minute or so later we caught up with the red car at the lights. The two vehicles stood side by side waiting for green to appear, the young man gunning his engine impressively as he prepared to accelerate away. My taxi driver turned to address me through the sliding glass partition that separated us.

'Excuse me, sir,' he said politely, 'I'm just going to swear at this person.'

Turning away from me, he leaned through the window beside him, and unleashed a pack of expressions that were breathtaking in their inventive and powerful use of every swear word that I have ever heard. He even managed to split up two- and three-syllable words in order to insert these pulses of invective. It was a masterful performance. The young man paled visibly and shrunk even lower in his

driving seat, crushed by the weight of such a profession-
ally executed attack.

Having expressed himself to his own complete satisfaction, my driver withdrew his head, turned around, and
addressed me once again in exactly the same tone of quiet
courtesy that he had used before.

'Sorry about that, sir,' he said, with the air of one
who has performed an unpleasant but necessary task as
efficiently as possible.

I was fascinated. He used the swearing pedal with the same dispassionate skill and selectivity as he operated the clutch or the brake or the accelerator. Unemotional invective was simply a tool of his trade. I used to think that I was like that driver – or at least – I *wanted* to be like him. I wanted to be in perfect control of every word and feeling and action at all times. A little careful adjustment of the appropriate pedal, at crucial moments, and no one need ever read a single page of the unedited version of Richard Norman Craven. Edna knew me inside-out, of course, but I didn't mind that. It was the rest of the world that was never going to be allowed to see the purple passages.

That's why I found it so difficult to read Dot's very frank description of my uncloaking. I actually blushed as I sat at home on my own, seeing my inanities mercilessly recorded on paper, together with the emotional outbursts that led to such a strange experience kneeling at the altar with Nunc. And there's another thing! How was it that I, a so-called writer of science fiction, accepted the presence of this extraordinary, non-human being as if he was a local at 'The Dog and Bucket'? I think, on reflection, that there were two reasons for that.

First, Nunc had his own very powerful aura of ordinariness. Unaccountable things happened when we were with him, but as a personality and a presence he was immediately familiar and integrated with everything else. He was just – Nunc.

The other thing was that after experiencing very profound and life-changing moments in the course of a Thrusday evening, the subsequent impact on day-to-day living was more residual than total.

On the evening after splurging my entrails all over

St Wilfred's for instance, I arrive home feeling bruised and battered in a positive sort of way, and expecting that, at the very least, God would be sitting in the armchair by the desk in my study, waiting to have a cosy chat with R. Craven about his bright spiritual future. In fact, when I did finally settle down with a hot chocolate, the angle-poise lamp, and my Jerusalem Bible, all I felt was an unusual quiet in my heart or mind, or wherever the noise usually blots out any chance of peace. Something had created a space, and I wondered how to fill it. In the end I remembered what Nunc had said about acknowledging my transgressions, so I tore a fresh sheet from one of the pads of A4, feint, narrow-line, margined paper that I carelessly buy for writing purposes, and started to list my faults and vices and shortcomings. After a bit it began to look like an outline for one of those television series that have to be shown on a Sunday night on Channel 4. I didn't like it, but I was not intimidated by it any more. When it was, at last, truly incomplete, I slapped it down on the desk, and for the first time in my life, I knelt down in my own study and tried to speak to God from the secret centre of myself.

'God,' I said, 'another prodigal here, only not quite as sure about coming home as the one in the story. I'm sorry about all the things on that list, and all the things that aren't on that list. I'm especially sorry about calling you nasty and narrow. When I think about Jesus in the garden wanting so much to stay alive, and all the stuff after that, I – well, I am *so* sorry. And I want to say thank you – I do hope you're listening, God, because this one's not easy – I want to say thank you for making my darling Edna so happy despite all that bl-dreadful illness, and I want to be absolutely honest and tell you that my stomach still knots up with anger when I think about it, but I guess yours probably does as well, so . . .'

The next bit *really* came from the heart.

'Lord, please don't let me become religious. Please don't let me pretend things and speak in a funny voice and put people off because I act like a weirdo. Let me go on being me, and I might end up being something for you.'

I said a lot of other things that I'm certainly not going to write down here, but I will record the last thing I said, although it makes my toes curl with embarrassment even to think about it. I guess it was the most important bit.

'Father – please – for Jesus' sake, don't leave me behind.'

Nothing very dramatic happened when I stood up, but in some secret part of myself, a small but perfectly formed Richard Craven leaped and skipped and flung his hat in the air. That night, as I yawned my way into bed, I was looking forward to two things. The first was the prospect of reading the Bible from a positive point of view. I decided to read a psalm a day, on the basis that it must keep something or other away, and I might even enjoy it. The second was the prospect of witnessing David Persimmon's attempt to spread light and joy in the general direction of Nigel Forsyth. I slept well.

The next morning I got up early and walked through the estate behind my house to the cemetery. I didn't go up there now as much as I had done, but I still experienced a feeling of sad peacefulness whenever I stood by the grave and said a few words to my sister. This morning there was something new to say.

'Edna, old girl,' I said softly, 'I reckon the need has just about come up level with the stubbornness, or it might even have got its nose in front. Anyway, the race is on!'

2

When David Persimmon asked me to write this chapter in the Nunc chronicles, he said that he wanted a clear record of what happened on the Thursday evening following the one that Dot described.

'Although,' he added, 'if I said or did anything foolish you can leave it out, and I'm the Vicar, so do as you're told.'

I pointed out as gently as I could that if I obeyed this instruction he would not appear in my section at all, but he said he was not amused, and would excommunicate me if I was rude about him. I would like to begin, therefore, by describing how, after my 'dessert fathers' triumph, I managed to catch Persimmon for the second time in a row, an achievement of which I am justly proud.

I was a little nervous about the evening in question in any case. Nigel Forsyth had, for some reason, postponed our friendly dinner party until the following week, and because of this and some thoughtless expiring on the part of one or two secular parishioners, Dave and I had made no contact (other than a brief telephone call) during the seven days since our last meeting. I was worried about how to behave. Having got so angry with David for daring to make progress in his spiritual life, I was now in the same position as he had been, and wondering if I ought to role-play ecstatic joy and crinkly-eyed evangelical warmth when I encountered everyone in the church. A slight lightening of the spirit seemed a very poor harvest from the dramatic emotional and spiritual scything of the week before. Wouldn't Dave and the others be rather disappointed to find that Craven Mark 2 was so little changed from the original model?

It was pouring with rain as I got ready to go out that evening. I didn't mind. I love rain. It sends all the weather-haters scurrying into their shelters, leaving the wonderful, wet world to me. I dragged my absurdly huge, blue and yellow golfing umbrella out of the cupboard under the stairs, opened the front door and stood for a moment on the step, wrestling with the umbrella's opening mechanism, and silently rehearsing the things I might say when I arrived at St Wilfred's. Five minutes later, after making my pleasantly melancholic way through a virtually deserted town, I shook my umbrella outside the church porch, leaned it against the wall in a corner, and pushed the inner door open.

There they sat in the familiar circle, three people and one alien who knew more about Richard Craven than the whole of the rest of the world put together. There was something about the empty chair placed in readiness for me that both warmed and embarrassed me. I was wanted and expected – but who was I?

The atmosphere was a little stiffer than usual from the start. Nunc, who had arrived on a stormy, wet night just like this one, made us all laugh just after I arrived when he said rather mournfully, 'As it was in the beginning, is now, and ever shall be, rain without end, amen,' but after that the dreaded moment arrived.

'Was it not wonderful, last week, Richard?' enthused Dot in a sort of second-rate actress's voice, 'truly wonderful.'

God help me, I felt my face contracting and twisting into the kind of simpering, pre-vomit expression that the situation seemed to demand.

'It was a great blessing, Dot,' I heard my mouth saying, 'I can't describe the joy! And the err . . . the feeling that I err . . . felt, because of – the joy . . .'

There was an uncomfortable silence. Dave was looking at me with knitted brows, clearly wondering whether it was safe to be himself. I remembered with a stab of shame the hard time I had given him last Thursday, but there was nothing I could do now. I was locked firmly into Christian mode.

'How have things been through the week, Dick?' he asked, following Dot's lead in amateur Shakespearean delivery. 'I would have popped in, but there was lots on, and, as I told you on the phone, I've been busier than I thought, burying err . . .'

'Dead people,' supplied Hartley helpfully, as though the Vicar was not quite able to recall whether the folk he had consigned to the cold earth were alive or deceased.

'I'm pretty sure they were dead, Hartley,' said David, then with a flash of his usual spirit, 'I reckon they dug the undertaker up specially for the occasion as well.'

We all tittered co-operatively except Nunc, whose eyes were far away.

'It's been a great week, Dave,' I bleated. 'I really feel I'm walking in the way, in a way that I haven't walked in it before . . .' There was a pause. 'I've confessed to lots of sins,' I added pathetically, 'ah, yes, and I'm reading a psalm every day, and err . . . meditating on it and finding it – I mean, them – a great blessing, or blessings, should I say? More than one blessing, I mean . . . and err . . . God is really real in a way that he wasn't. Well, he was, but I thought he wasn't if you see what I mean . . .'

I swallowed with difficulty. What on earth was going on? Last week I might have been a confused and hard-hearted pagan, but at least I'd been able to address other people without sounding like some badly written, human tract. I recalled my prayer a week ago about not speaking in a funny voice, and it was then that I decided it was time for Reverend Persimmon to be led up the garden path for the second time. I knew that Dot thoroughly disapproves of the game that Dave and I play occasionally, but, on this occasion it seemed like the only way out of the paralysed situation that I felt I'd got the group into.

'Dave,' I said, my voice much firmer than before, 'one of the sins I had to confess to was pride and intolerance.'

Dave and Dot almost fell off their seats in their eagerness to reassure me that I was not alone in my transgressions.

'I think we all suffer from that shortcoming,' encouraged Dot, who is one of the least proud people I know.

'Or some other sin,' said Persimmon, who is easily the most intolerant person I have ever met.

'I take buns,' said Hartley, putting me off my stroke momentarily, 'but not since coming to Mrs Bletchley's because there is a snack shelf provided for those who are hungry between meals.'

'What a very good idea,' said Dot, 'so thoughtful.'

'Anyway,' I continued doggedly, 'I thought back over the last few years, and I realized how downright rude and, frankly, unpleasant I'd been about things that meant a lot to other people. For instance, do you remember last

Christmas when Felicity Ray organized a Christmas dance for the church at Witley Hall?'

'Oh, yes,' grunted David, 'one of those awful events where someone shouts out:

> Turn your partners, bring them back,
> Make your feet go whickety-whack!

The church's dancing equivalent to quiche; yes, I remember. I reckon she only suggested it because she knew I wasn't keen. She's never been keen on me since the time when Bert Ray fancied her but was too shy to say anything, and I said in the group one evening that I felt led to say a prayer for Bert straight from the prayer book, and he said "What?" and I said, "It's a prayer asking that you should attain everlasting joy and Felicity," and she went bright red. Mind you, it did the trick, and –'

'Could I finish, Dave?' I interrupted. 'I'm talking about what God's been doing in my life this week, and you're going on about something you said to somebody about –'

'Sorry, Dick,' said David, that same tense frown appearing on his face, 'carry on with what you were saying.'

'Well, I was just going to say that I remembered how scathing I'd been about Felicity's efforts, saying it was a typical, bland church activity, and then, when I went to the dance and Dot, among others, forced me to join in, I found to my horror that I really enjoyed it.'

'Of course you did!' said Dot briskly.

'So did I!' said Hartley.

'I realized this week that I never really apologized to Felicity for being so negative. And what I wanted to share with you, Dave – '

'*Share* with me?' repeated Dave, as though I'd given him a slice of lemon to suck.

'What I wanted to share with you was that, this week, when I was reading my Bible, I suddenly came across a verse that convicted me – '

'*Convicted* you?' echoed Dave, biting into that lemon again. 'Why on earth are you – '

'It convicted me of my error in condemning that particular activity and made me realize that the Lord would have me repent.'

'Do you mean he *wants* you to repent? What do you mean, he would *have* you repent? Can't he speak normal English?'

By now I had my face well under control. I gave Dave the most sickly, unpleasantly forgiving smile that I could manage.

'Do you want to know what the verse was, Dave?' I enquired with oily patience, 'or would you rather we moved into a time of worship now?'

'I don't want to move into anything,' said David gloomily, 'and you'd better tell me what the blasted verse is, or you'll decide you have to deliver me from the demon of boredom.'

I laughed in a controlled, charitable manner, as though to encourage a weaker brother. He gnashed his teeth.

'Well?' he growled, 'get on with it – the second coming's due any moment now.'

'What was this verse, Richard?' asked Dot, who was looking at me in a very puzzled way. Hardly surprising in the circumstances.

'This is it,' I said, opening my Bible and pointing at

some lines on the page. 'I'll read it to you. "I am come that they might have life, and have it in a barn-dance . . ."'

Another of Dot's flying-bomb silences fell at this point, and Dave's face was working away like a couple of moles under a sheet. Bearing in mind his violent physical attack after my scholarly exposition of the history of the 'dessert fathers', I braced myself for another battle, but it was not to be. Dave slumped back in his chair and passed a hand across his brow as if wiping away perspiration. He expelled air noisily from inflated cheeks.

'Well, thank goodness for that! I really thought you'd joined the ranks of the happy-clappers for a minute there.'

'When I worship at Bowden Road,' said Dot severely, 'I clap, and I am very happy. May I ask what is wrong with that?'

'Sorry, Dot,' said Dave, 'there's nothing wrong with that. It was just shorthand. I was so relieved to find that Dick hadn't disappeared into the divine funny-farm, that . . . blimey, Dick, you really had me going there.'

'I had *myself* going when I first got here,' I admitted. 'It was last week, you see. After what happened I felt the least I could do was walk in with a springy step and shiny eyes, even if that wasn't really how I felt. Then I thought how stupid that was. After all, Dot's always herself, and you never cover up the fact that you're an awkward, cantankerous old cuss, do you, Dave?'

'No, Dick, it's very kind of you to point that out – thank you.'

'And the only way I could think of to get back to normal was to have you on a bit. The trouble is, there isn't a language for the way things really are. It all sounds so cringe-worthy. What's your average character in the street going to make of me talking about a "mighty counsellor in the church militant"?'

'I s'pose they'll assume that Derek Hatton's been converted,' said Dave brightly.

'Surely,' said Dot, wriggling slightly on her chair with the sheer intensity of her feelings, 'you just speak from your heart about the things that are really true for you – don't you? That's what I do.'

'It's true for you, Dot,' said David, 'but that's because you're made that way. If you say, "Jesus took my sins away, and now I'm h-a-p-p-y" it sounds genuine because it's part of you, but Dick and I can't do it. I pretend to be blunt and straightforward, but I'm not really, and Dick's about as straight as a French horn.'

I raised a hand in mock-acknowledgement. 'My turn to thank *you*, Vicar,' I said, 'what a wonderful recommendation.'

Hartley cleared his throat nervously before speaking.

'I told Mrs Bletchley that I needed to have an early tea because if I did not I would become institutionalized, but really it was because I wanted to see Nunc before anyone else came two weeks ago, but I think she knew what I was really thinking because she asked me what happened at Mr Mountford's, and when I told her that he called me a cross-eyed freak she said I could have an early tea whenever I had a good reason, so I could have just asked her in the first place, and I wish I had. What sort of instrument do you think I am like, Reverend Persimmon?'

We were all stunned for a few moments by this unusually long speech, but it was okay – David is very fond of Hartley.

'Hartley,' he said gently, 'I'd say you were like one of those marvellous alpine horns, just a very gentle curve, but otherwise quite straight.'

Hartley's pleased grin was wonderful.

'Tell us how your life has changed since last week, Richard.' As usual, Nunc's voice redirected events like the beginning of a new page.

'And I pray and beseech you to tell only the truth.'

The truth! He wanted me to tell the truth, but even as the words sunk in, I realized how many pressures there were on me to tell anything but the truth. I wanted to exaggerate for God. Why should he be given a poor reference? I wanted to exaggerate for myself. Surely there would be an element of self-fulfilling prophecy in extravagant claims? I wanted to exaggerate for Hartley. After the ragged displays he'd seen from Dave and me over the last couple of weeks, didn't he deserve to hear something solid and admirable? I wanted to exaggerate for the whole of the universe. What use was Christianity to creation if its manifestation in me boiled down to some pathetically thin testimony? I wanted to exaggerate for Nunc. He had led me into the most beautiful experience of my life last week – why should I not give the impression that the wonder of those few short minutes had continued to be part of my life?

In the end I told the truth because (I promise I'm not mad) I saw in my mind, as if it was an extract from a film, a vision of Peter the disciple, leaning miserably against a courtyard wall, the wretchedness in his eyes all too apparent in the flickering light from an open fire. And I suddenly knew, although I'd never really thought about it before, that a large part of his denial of Jesus had been not just fear, but embarrassment about the apparent weakness and failure of the man he had followed for three years. Perhaps he chose between exaggeration or denial – who knows?

'How has my life changed?' I repeated Nunc's question as these thoughts went through my mind, and all at once I knew what the truth was. 'Every single day since last Thursday,' I said, 'I have wanted to get up in the morning. That is the truth.'

Knowing David Persimmon as I do, I was not at all surprised or shocked by his reaction to this rather undramatic statement.

'Well, Glory hallelujah!' he cried, shooting to his feet and waving his hands in the air like some music-hall revivalist. 'Praise the Lord! Praise his almighty name for he has done marvellous and wonderful things! Richard Craven wants to get up in the morning! All of creation rejoices in this wondrous miracle! Hallelujah!'

He began to execute an absurd, hopping dance around the outside of our circle, clapping his hands with deliberate inaccuracy and singing 'Bringing in the sheaves' in a sort of wobbling pentecostal tenor. Understanding that this response was largely motivated by relief at discovering that I had not, after all, departed from the land of the normal, I was not at all upset – in fact, I laughed. Dear Dot was not at all amused, however.

'David Persimmon!' she snapped, like an infant teacher who has caught one of her charges doing something disgusting in the washrooms, 'stop that immediately! When will you learn? Just how old do you think you are?'

For all his height and bulk, Dave looked just like a naughty child as he stopped dancing, hung his head and replied to Dot.

'I'm so old,' he said, 'that I can remember when athletes took monoids instead of steroids. I should know better, but my education was muffed when I was a little chap, and –'

'This is no time for joking, David,' interrupted Dot sharply. 'Richard was saying something very serious indeed.'

Impressed by the authority and severity of Dot's manner, we all fell silent, obediently contemplating the seriousness of what I had said. Poor old Hartley broke the spell in the end by bursting into a fit of giggles, just as he had after I'd read out the Vicar's 'worm' prophecy. David and I lasted another one and a half seconds before we collapsed into helpless laughter. Nunc smiled.

'I really do fail to understand you two men sometimes,' said Dot, looking from Dave to me and back again in bewilderment. 'One minute you react with the most fragile sensitivity, and the next you seem to be finding quite crass and unsympathetic behaviour screamingly funny.'

'I'm sorry, Dot,' I apologized, wiping my eyes with a handkerchief, 'it's just that we're both so relieved to discover that there's life after revival. We're still friends and that's worth an awful lot. But you're right, I *was* saying something very serious and I hadn't even really seen it until just now. You see, ever since Edna died I've woken up every morning – nearly every morning – with a shadow over me. That's putting it politely. More often than not I'd open my eyes and say, "Oh, sugar! Another stinking day!" That's why your coming here was such a relief to me, Dave. Whenever I knew we were going to spend some time together, preferably in some pagan eating-house in a remote corner of the town, I quite looked forward to being fully conscious. Like you said, we've always joked, we've always sparked each other off. But that's one of the few things that have seemed worth getting up for. Even the exploits of Elmed Brarg and the mighty Vorgans only stimulated me occasionally, and because I have to eat. There was always a heaviness – a greyness. But this week – '

'Why didn't you ever tell me about Edna, you rat?' demanded Dave, expressing his hurt through aggression as usual.

I was ready for that one.

'Why didn't you tell me that you'd been an unhappy little boy who heard his world falling apart on the other side of the door, you pig?'

'Yes, David,' said Dot, 'you have never spoken to *me* about that part of your life, have you?'

'You have been a bit of a Thompson's gazelle,' said Hartley, with such gravity that Dave and I burst into laughter again.

Dot cleared her throat eloquently in our direction.

'Yes, well,' said Dave, sprawling down on the front pew, 'if this zoological analysis of my autobiographical reticence is more or less complete – ' I rewarded this effusion with a short round of applause '– you were saying something about this week, Dick?'

'This week,' I continued, 'it's been different. I don't mean I've been leaping out of bed like a jack-in-the-box, but I have been keen to find out what's going to happen. I feel lighter, much more part of things – I can *see* things again.'

'Could you not see things before this week, Mr Craven?'

'I wasn't blind, Hartley, no, but I'd stopped seeing colours and shape and textures. I was living in a little dark world inside myself and I didn't want to come out. Now – well, I suppose the world seems a bit brighter and better. I'm quite enjoying reading the old psalms, and when I pray I feel as if I'm really talking to someone. But the real difference is this wanting to be alive – wanting to wake up. It sounds like nothing but it's a huge difference.'

Dave sighed deeply. 'You're way ahead of me, Dick. I've only got as far as deciding to start again.' Something struck him. 'Here, you're going to have to beef your testimony up for the old clean-necked brigade, aren't you? "World seems a bit brighter and better?" You might get into heaven with that, but it won't get you on the platform at Spring Harvest. One of your greatest ambitions, isn't it, Dick? I can just see you doing one of those little on-the-spot dances in the big-top. And you could do a seminar about waking up in the morning, followed later in the year by a helpful little paperback entitled *Alarm Clock for God – the Craven way to full spiritual health*. The possibilities are endless.'

'I find what has happened to Richard quite wonderful enough without any "beefing up", as you put it, David. And may I ask whether you consider my neck to be less than clean?'

'As clean as a Jimmy White pot, Dot,' replied Dave promptly.

Dot beamed happily – she's a tremendous snooker fan.

'Just one more thing about your entrail-display last week,' said Dave. 'What about the long speech you gave us on the subject of children's literature? Was that all defensive baloney, or did you mean some of it?'

I walked over and placed a hand on Dave's shoulder.

'Reverend Persimmon,' I said humbly, 'you have a wonderful ministry of encouragement. Did you really think it sounded like defensive baloney, or are you just saying that?'

'I am aware that you are attempting to be satirical, Craven, but I shall answer you anyway, because I have a more charitable spirit than you. First of all, I do not have a ministry of encouragement and I do not want one. William Critchely has a ministry of encouragement. He is a menace. I remember once I met him by the hall door as he was about to go in for his prophetic macramé group, or whatever it was, and I opened the door for him. He thanked me as if I'd saved his life at sea, and told me that I had a "gift of enabling". Last month he stood up in church, smiled all over everybody, and said that he just wanted to share with all of us that Jimmy Pratchett, who, as you know, is one of the nicest and most cack-handed people in the universe, had helped to repaint the hall – probably made the tea. And, said Critchely, he had a real gift of decorating, would you believe? After the service old Mrs Sipley asked Jimmy to come round and paper her living room for her. Poor old Jimmy, puzzled but convinced about his "gift for decorating", goes round and creates the most comprehensively glue-ridden disaster zone I have ever seen in my life.

'I took it upon myself to go round and ask William Critchely if he had a gift of compensating. He wasn't sure, but after some fairly aggressive encouragement from me, he decided he probably had. He now has a ministry of encouragement that's a little more selective and much more truthful – a bit less expensive as well . . .

'Secondly, I didn't think what you said sounded like defensive baloney, which is, of course, why I said it did. I thought it sounded quite interesting, considering its source. So was it or wasn't it?'

David Persimmon makes my head spin sometimes. I sat down on the pew next to him and thought about his question.

'Yes,' I decided, 'I did mean what I said. I'm not exactly sure what an adventure is, but I reckon there are probably as many different kinds of experience as there are Christians. This last week hasn't been an adventure for me – it's been . . . well, it's been the beginning of peace. Dot's life has been an adventure, your life is a series of accidental breakages, Dave, and Hartley's life is – what is your life, Hartley? Are you on an adventure?'

Hartley usually stays very placid, but when I asked him this question he leaned forward excitedly in his chair, his eyes shining, and rubbed his hands together with anticipatory glee.

'Can we tell them now, Nunc?' he asked.

'Now is the acceptable time,' answered Nunc, 'tell them, Hartley.'

'The thing is,' said Hartley, 'that late last night when nobody else was in the church, we – I mean Nunc and I – we *had* an adventure! Do you want to hear about it?'

'We certainly do,' enthused Dot, 'how very intriguing!'

3

'We were sitting just here when the car stopped!'

It was five minutes later. Hartley had insisted on shepherding us all into the main porch, where, through the open outer door, we could see that the rain was still beating down. It felt cosy to be sitting in the dry porch watching the weather as if it was a television programme. Outside the front door a flight of shallow steps descended to a brick pavement, while on the other side of the road another, narrower set of steps led up to a gravel path that ran beside and above the roadway. Immediately opposite us, next to the gravel path, stood an old-fashioned red telephone box, and, beside it, a streetlamp cast a yellow glow over the whole scene. It was an oddly artificial, theatrical effect, like those unconvincing B-movie film sets that were common in the sixties. Hartley stood proprietorially just inside the front door, his face alight with memory.

'It was exactly like this,' he said, 'except that it was much later. I came at seven o'clock to do some cleaning and see Nunc, but the rain started at nine-thirty as I was about to leave, and I had not brought an umbrella because I do not have an umbrella, and I had not brought a coat because I am very silly, so – I hope it was all right, Reverened Persimmon – I telephoned Mrs Bletchley from the vestry to say that I would be late and she said not to worry because she would leave the key under the flat stone that we use . . .'

'Good idea to use the phone, Hartley,' nodded Dave, as Hartley paused for breath, 'good thinking.'

'For a while,' continued Hartley, 'Nunc and I talked about what we both like to eat most. I said that my favourite food was bacon sandwiches with thick butter, and Nunc said that he does not eat any of the things that we have, but that Reverend Persimmon would know what he *does* eat, because it is the same as our founder's favourite food.'

We all looked expectantly at Dave, who looked utterly blank. Several seconds passed. The Vicar squirmed irritably.

'Knock, knock!' he said at last, quite inexplicably.

I sighed. 'Who's there?'

'Armageddon,' replied Dave.

'Armageddon who?' I wearily enquired.

'Armageddon tired of you all watching me wondering what on earth Nunc is talking about . . .'

'The person at the well,' murmured Nunc softly.

'I'll work it out later,' said Dave, 'you go on with your story, Hartley.'

Dot and I were sitting on the stone bench at one side of the porch, and Dave and Nunc at the other. Hartley now left his post at the door, sat down close to Dot, who was looking a little shivery, and went on with his story.

'After we had discussed food we went into the hall to play with the crèche toys – Nunc pedalled a small car, and I wore a tiny policeman's helmet made of cardboard and attached round my chin with a rubber band.'

'I was arrested five times and fined a total of fifteen coloured wooden bricks,' added Nunc seriously, 'it was a wonderful game. No wonder Hartley is the most important person in the Church of England. He is a very, very good person to play with.'

'Then we decided to go and see if the weather was any better,' said Hartley. 'Nunc is not allowed to go out of the building, of course, but he said it would be permissible to sit in the porch and look out, so we sat almost exactly where we are sitting now, and we watched cars going past, down on the lane. We enjoyed seeing the lights before the cars arrived, and hearing the wet, whizzing noise their tyres made on the road. The rain looked as if it was never going to end, and I was glad because it felt extremely exciting to be out so late, and extremely safe as well because Mrs Bletchley had said that I need not worry about being late. But then something happened, and for a little while I was quite frightened.'

'One of the cars stopped,' said Nunc, 'instead of whizzing past.'

'Yes!' breathed Hartley, the panic of that moment returning as he verbally replayed the experience. 'It stopped! I did not think it was a car that was coming because of the noise that the engine made. It sounded like a tractor or some other big thing. But when it came into view and stopped under the light on the other side of the road I saw that it was just an ordinary car, and I realized there must be something wrong with the engine.'

'Why were you worried about the car stopping, Hartley?'

Hartley's brow creased. 'I am not exactly sure, Dot, except that by then it was very late and I was not at home. I was very excited, as I said just now, but – well, when you have been told off for most of your life, you feel sure that it will happen again, especially when you are feeling happy. I know that it might sound strange, but I was afraid that the man in the car might be someone from the council who had come to drag me home. That has happened to me before, when they would not believe that Mr Kemp hit me every evening with a wet towel when I was a small boy, and I hid in a bus shelter for half a night and pretended that someone would soon come to take me home, to a place with a three-piece suite and soft carpet and a clock ticking and a room of my own with Manchester United posters, and people with the same second name as me who were not staff.'

A sudden gust of wind rattled and whistled through the tiled roof of the old porch. Dot placed her arm around Hartley's shoulders and Nunc glowed, not only with light this time, but with a gentle, very welcome warmth as well.

'By golly!' exclaimed Dave, wiping something from his eye as he spoke, 'if you'd only let me market you as a space-age, multi-functional appliance, Nunc, we'd make a fortune.'

'I am happy to provide light for them that sit in darkness,' smiled Nunc, 'but I would not court poverty by selling what is mine to give.'

'Carry on with the story, Hartley,' I said, 'the car stopped – what happened next?'

'Yes, it stopped, and after a minute or two a man got out holding a torch, and he hurried up the steps on the opposite side of the road and went into the telephone box. He stayed in there for quite a long time before coming out and going back to his car. He opened the door on the driver's side, and was just about to climb inside when he turned his head and looked straight up at the porch where we were sitting. He stood stock-still for a moment as if he was making up his mind what to do, and then he leaned into his car, pulled out a briefcase and shut the door again.'

I swear that Hartley's hair stood on end as he continued to speak.

'We had the porch light on last night,' he said, pointing at the bare lightbulb that hung from the rafters above us, 'so he must have seen that when he looked up – the porch all lit up, I mean – and he ran across the lane with his coat over his head and he jumped up the steps and was suddenly in the porch – here – before we could move or do anything about it. I was too frightened to move at first. I had a dreadful fear that when the man took his coat off his head he would have the face of an eagle or a wart-hog or a hyena, but when he did take it off he looked quite normal except for his purple vest.'

'Purple vest?' said Dave, screwing his face up in puzzlement, 'must have been a sixties freak – or a bishop,' he added, laughing heartily at his own joke.

'He also had a collar a bit like yours only smaller, Reverend Persimmon.'

If ever a cleaning company develops a product that wipes away dirt as quickly and completely as that remark of Hartley's wiped the smile from Persimmon's face, they would very swiftly be in conflict with the Monopolies Commission.

'He had a *what*?'

'A collar a bit like yours,' repeated Hartley stolidly, 'except that his looked cleaner and straighter even though he had been running across the road and up the steps with his coat on his head, which seems strange because – '

'All right, Hartley,' said Dave, 'the man had a wonderful collar. Anything else? What did he look like? How big was he? What was his name? Where did he come from?'

'I am not clever at judging people's heights,' said Hartley, in response to this barrage of questions, 'he was not very tall or very small and he was not a fat man. His stomach did not come out at the front in the way that yours does, Reverend Persimmon – '

'Oh good . . .' grunted Dave.

'And he was wearing a grey suit over his purple vest, and black shoes. He was rather bald on top with grey hair at the sides, and he had a sort of oblong face and glasses that he took off and wiped when he came in.' Hartley thought for a moment. 'Oh, and one other thing – he had a gap in his teeth, at the top – here.' Hartley tapped the middle of his top teeth with a forefinger.

Dave and Dot and I looked at each other like a trio of stout Cortezes gazing at the Pacific for the first time, but none of us said anything – then.

'Go on, Hartley,' said Dave, in a voice that was – for him – unusually quiet and curious, 'what happened next?'

'Well,' answered Hartley, 'the man did a little jump backwards when he saw me, then he finished cleaning his glasses and looked at me. He said, "Well, good evening, I never expected to find anyone sitting in a place like this on such a dreadful night. My car's playing up so I stopped over there to phone for help".'

Hartley strained to remember something.

'The man did tell me who he was calling, Reverend Persimmon, but they were two rather long words and I cannot recall what they were, I'm afraid.'

'It's okay, Hartley,' Dave flapped a hand reassuringly, 'I reckon we can guess who he rang. It was probably that well-known organization staffed by very, very nice men who sometimes take a very, very long time to arrive. Carry on . . .'

'He had a nice voice and he looked kind, so I stopped feeling frightened, especially as he shook my hand very politely and asked what my name was. I told him I was called Hartley and that I lived at Mrs Bletchley's hostel or home, and he wanted to know if I was a member of this church, but just as I was about to answer him, Nunc, whom he had not yet seen because he was sitting where he is now on the other side of the porch, interrupted what I was saying.'

'What did Nunc say?' asked Dot, deeply interested, as we all were.

'He said, "Hartley is the most important person in the Church of England," and the man spun round like a top, saw Nunc and said "Good heavens!"'

Dave looked puzzled. 'I thought Nunc said we were the only people who could see him – didn't you, Nunc?'

'I said that four or five people would be able to see or hear me,' replied Nunc, 'this man was the fifth. When he turned to face me he looked a little shocked, so I said distinctly, with an audible voice, "Good evening, my name is Nunc and I am an alien, waiting here at St Wilfred's for a matter of weeks. My friend Hartley cleans and tidies the inner part of the building, and, as I have already stated, he is the most important person in the Church of England."

'Our visitor sank onto the bench beside Hartley, looking distinctly confused as he inwardly digested this information, but after only a few moments, during which he shook his head as if to clear it, he came over to take my hand, and said, "You really must excuse my bad manners. You see, I've never met an alien before. It's wonderful to meet you, Nunc." He then returned to his seat and gazed from Hartley to myself and back again to Hartley, again and again.'

Hartley took up the story once more.

'I said to the man that I thought he looked very tired, and he said that he had not very long since begun a new and very difficult job, and it did make him feel rather tired sometimes, especially as people kept moving the goalposts. When I asked him if he was a football player he laughed and said he had really meant that just as you think you might have done quite well with one thing, it turns out that people are cross with you for not doing something completely different. I asked him if it was like a day I remember at Mr Mountford's, when I spent all Saturday mowing the lawn so that he would be pleased with me, and when he came back at teatime he told me off because I had left my pyjama trousers on the floor of my bedroom, and he did not even notice that I had done the lawn. He said it was exactly, precisely, absolutely like that in his job, and he also said that it was a bit like being the manager of Liverpool *and* Manchester United when they play at Wembley.

'Then he looked at Nunc and me and smiled.

'"An alien and the most important person in the Church of England, eh? What an interesting coincidence."

'"Are you also an alien, then?" asked Nunc very quietly.

'"Well, that's partly what I mean," said the man. "I do quite often feel, in this job I have, that people make me into a sort of alien. They behave very oddly when they meet me sometimes – as though I'd come from a different planet."

'"You do not really look like an alien," I said, hoping to encourage.

'"Ah, you should see me sometimes," chuckled the man, "you might change your mind about that – you might indeed!"

'"What was the other part of the coincidence, sir?" I asked.

'The man stood up and walked over to the door. He

leaned against the stone archway and stared out into the rain as he spoke.

'"The other part of the coincidence is that, whereas you are the most important person in the Church of England, Hartley, I am the *least* important person in that great institution, and the responsibility weighs very heavily on me at times."

'"Who told you that you are the least important person in the church?" I enquired. He did not seem an unimportant person.

'"The only person who really knows – that's who told me," said the man, in a funny, happy-sad sort of voice. "The trouble is, I'm not always very good at washing feet."

'"Is that what you do, then?" – I was really surprised – "you wash feet for a living?"

'"I do what I'm told – or I try to," he said, "and if it ever involves washing the odd foot – well, it goes with the job."

'He turned round towards us again then, and looked at Nunc, who was just beginning to shine. "What do you think, Nunc?" he asked, "am I going to make it, do you reckon?"

'"In your new job?"

'"Yes, in my new job."

'"I think," said Nunc mildly, "that it would be very dangerous to wash a man's feet when everything in you wants to empty the bowl of water over his head. I cannot recall your founder offering to wash the feet of the Pharisees. Was he not openly and quite scathingly angry with them? Was he not correspondingly tender and compassionate with sinners who knew that they were far from perfect? Anger and love, and something in-between that was steady, straight and grown-up. Hartley tells me that you humans use the word 'twit', meaning a very silly, non-serious person. I believe I am right in saying that your holy writings exhort you to be 'fools for Christ'. There is, if I may say so, a big difference between being a fool for Christ and a 'twit for Christ'. A fool may die socially or intellectually or physically, because he knows that, in another context, his foolishness will be revealed as wisdom."

"'And a twit?" asked the man.

"'A twit," said Nunc, "will flit from one point of view to another, putting more energy into his effort to avoid offending than into anything else. People who should be exploded at, will have their feet washed, and tired folk who know they are probably wrong will be told to be patient and learn to control themselves."

"'And what am I?" queried the man, a strange little smile playing around his lips, "a fool or a twit?"

'Nunc looked at him very seriously. "You have a lot of anger and a lot of love in you," he said, "pray for the strength to use them as an obedient fool would, whether such use leads to acclamation or crucifixion."

"'Well, I shall – "

'Whatever the man had been about to say was interrupted by a swish of tyres as a large van, one with an orange light on top, pulled into the space in front of the car opposite and stopped. A man dressed in cape and waterproof trousers got out and walked back to our visitor's car.

"'I must go," he said, then he shook hands with Nunc and me, and thanked us for our hospitality and said he hoped we'd all meet again. Just as he was about to go down the steps he stopped, looked at me for a moment, and said, "I promise I won't forget that you're the most important person in the Church of England, Hartley. Goodbye!"

'Nunc and I watched for quite a long time while the man in the cape did something under the bonnet of our visitor's car, then he tried the engine and it did not sound like a tractor any more. Soon after that both of the cars drove away, and the rain stopped so I went home. It was very late when I arrived home, but Mrs Bletchley had left the key under the stone, and she was still awake when I came in because she called out, "Is that you, Hartley?" and I called back, "Yes, it's me," and she said, "Sleep well, dear" and I did. But – ' Hartley was still quivering with excitement – 'it was quite an adventure, was it not?'

'It certainly was,' said Dave. 'Tell me, Hartley, did this balding, purple-vested, oblong-faced, gap-toothed character say anything else about . . . anything else?'

Hartley's eyeballs disappeared upwards as he tried to recall.

'I believe he said that he was expecting his car to confess its manifold sins to the mechanic when he arrived, but I think that was a joke and I did not really understand it.'

'Did he say what his name was, Hartley?' I asked. 'You must have called him *something*, surely?'

'I called him "Sir",' said Hartley. 'He was the sort of person whom you call "Sir" without anyone telling you that you should.'

'No name at all, then,' murmured Dot, more to herself than to anyone else. 'How very odd!'

'There was one thing.' Hartley sat up suddenly and raised his hand in the air as though he was answering a question in a junior class. 'He had a bag – a briefcase, made of leather, and there were two letters stamped on the front.'

'Initials you mean?' demanded Dave, leaning forward intently.

'I suppose so,' said Hartley blankly, 'the letters were G and C, I think.'

Dave, Dot and I did our stout Cortez act again, but, for some reason, I think we all knew that we would still not discuss the direction in which our thoughts were going, not until quite a lot of time had passed.

Dave leaned back and rubbed his chin thoughtfully.

'Hmm . . .' he said, 'could be Gregory Carstairs, or Geraint Cadwalader, or Grant Capstick, or Gavin Crunge . . .'

'Or Geoffrey Chamberlain,' I put in, 'or Gordon Camembert, or Godolphus Crane, or Galahad Culpepper, or Gertrude Cavanagh (if he'd borrowed his wife's bag, I mean), or Glyn Cashmir . . .'

'Or Graham Clingfilm,' said Dot, blushing slightly as she realized that she'd been drawn into flippancy.

'Do be serious, Dot,' admonished Dave annoyingly. 'How could anyone possibly be called Graham Clingfilm? Gungadin Cod, perhaps, or Geronimo Cattleburger, but Graham Clingfilm? I don't really think so, do you, Hartley?'

Hartley was staring out into the ever-worsening weather with a wistful expression on his face. 'I do not know what his name was,' he said, 'but I liked him and I would very much like to meet him again. I am not sure, when I think about it, that he can really have been the least important person in the Church of England. And I wonder what his new job was?'

Just then a car passed along the road outside, sending a spray of water up onto the bank beneath the telephone box. We all jumped a little and craned our necks towards the open doorway. For a moment I thought the car was going to stop, but it had only slowed to pass through the puddles at the side of the lane, and soon it accelerated away, until we could neither see nor hear it any more.

4

'Right, Craven, what about the old scribbling, then? Is it all "Vong the Vegan-slayer" stuff, or has your fresh desire to be conscious from time to time produced any new work?'

We had retired to the church hall, where a wall heater toasted us deliciously as we sat around it in a close semi-circle, our faces shimmering red in the glow from the gas-fire. We had decided to leave all the other hall lights out as we drank the inevitable coffee and cocoa. Our only extra potential illumination was a half-used household candle stuck on a coffee jar lid by our resourceful spiritual leader, and placed on a small wooden table borrowed from the vestry, where a wide range of obscure ecclesiastical furniture was stored. As Dave asked me about 'new work', he picked up one of the matches that he had just dropped over the floor, and finally managed to set fire to the blackened wick.

'As a matter of fact, Dave, I have been doing a little experimental "scribbling", as you put it. Not, I hasten to add, just because of your crude attempts to influence me, but primarily because my attitude to certain things has changed. In fact' – I must have sounded a little nervous –

'this week, for the first time for years, I actually wrote some verse. I won't dignify it by calling it poetry, but at least it's an attempt.'

'I think that's wonderful, Richard!' said Dot, her eyes shining with genuine pleasure in the candlelight. 'We'd love to hear what you've written, wouldn't we, everybody?'

She looked around confidently, to be rewarded with nods and noises of agreement from Nunc and Hartley. Persimmon, on the other hand, with his peculiar brand of insensitivity that can be equally engaging or infuriating, set off on one of his Mercutio-like monologues, apparently quite unaware that he was killing the moment.

'I've seen a lot of so-called Christian poetry,' he said loudly. 'Every now and then my parishioners express their feelings on grease-proof paper with a blunt pencil, then bring the results along to me, and tell me the Lord "gave them" this poem. When you read most of these offerings you can see why he gave them away – glad to be rid of 'em in most cases, if you ask me.'

'Richard was just about to – '

'Terrible doggerel, most of 'em,' continued the Vicar, drowning Dot's brave attempt to swim out and rescue the rest of what I had started to say, 'awful stuff that no one would even look at in the secular world. But it doesn't matter how bad it is, apparently, because it's "for the Lord". All I can say is that "the Lord" must be either very tolerant or completely lacking in taste. I'll give you an example of the sort of thing I mean . . .'

Dave leaned back and thrust both arms straight up into the air as he extemporized, unconscious of Dot's sigh of annoyance and frustration.

'Everyone ought to come to Jesus and be saved,
Even people who are really nasty and depraved.
It was nineteen eighty-three when I asked him into my life,
Closely followed, three weeks later, by my wife.

That's the sort of stuff I'm talking about. There are usually about a hundred verses, and the meter and rhymes get progressively worse as the thing goes on. The trouble is, you see, that the rhyme starts to dictate the meaning – '

'I wonder if Richard could just tell us about the verse that he has – '

But the Vicar was unstoppable.

'Let's say, for instance, that I write a line like "God speaks gently, God speaks sternly." I look at it for a while, tell myself what a very wonderful thing I've written, then try to work out a rhyme. 'Mernly, wernly, sernly, dernly, fernly, nernly – nothing seems to fit. Then, at last, I hit on something that works, and I end up with a couplet like this:

> God speaks gently, God speaks sternly,
> God speaks out to those in Burnley.

Then I recite it somewhere in bold tones and after a lengthy, depressed silence, one of the unfortunate recipients of my poetic genius says, "Why Burnley?" If I'm feeling honest I'll admit that it was the only word that rhymed, but if I'm in Mickey Mouse – mystical – mode I screw my eyes up, stare into the far distance, and say, "Ah, well, I just felt the Lord gave me a little nudge when I was writing that – I think something amazing is going to happen in Burnley very soon," and people are singularly unimpressed, especially if they come from Burnley. Can't blame them really, can you?'

There was a short silence. I nodded with judicial seriousness.

'Well, Reverend Persimmon,' I said, 'I would like to thank you on behalf of all those present for such an illuminating and profound analysis of Christian poetry in the twentieth century. I would like, additionally, to say a big personal thank you for your sensitive and large-hearted awareness of the fact that I wanted so much to be interrupted just as I was about to make a very tentative offering of something which you, more than anyone else, have encouraged me to produce. Please accept my sincere and effusive gratitude for your unusual thoughtfulness.'

'Are you trying to say something, Craven?' asked the Vicar calmly.

'Really David!' said Dot, unable to restrain herself any longer. 'I do not suppose that I shall ever understand the mysterious convolutions of your personality. You are like –' Dot paused, her lips tightly pursed, as she sought an appropriate simile ' – like some potter who, after hours of work, takes his creations out of the kiln and immediately smashes them against the wall for no apparent reason. You *knew* that you were interrupting Richard at a very important juncture – I am quite sure that you did. I find it most puzzling that you are able to give in to those weak impulses within yourself. You are incorrigible!'

'No I'm not,' said Dave sulkily, 'I'm Church of England. I don't know why I do it, Dot. Perhaps if my potty had played a little tune every time I "succeeded" I'd be a bit more confident about following things through . . . Seriously, I don't know why I do it. I get as worried about being right as I do about being wrong. Full of complexes, I am – like a raspberry ripple. I shall now repent.'

Nearly knocking over the table that supported our candle, he prostrated himself with absurd abandonment at my feet, and proceeded to repent.

'Oh, good, close, wise and wonderful friend,' he cringed, 'I humbly beg your valuable pardon for cutting you off in your thingummybob. Please be kind enough to favour us with the benefit of your recitations, or, if you see fit, cut your wretched servant's throat and let me die here at your feet. Whatever you decide – get on with it, there's a good chap. We haven't got much longer.'

He got up, dusted his knees, and sat down wearing the little-boy look that always brings out the mother hen in Dot.

'Well, am I forgiven?'

'Don't be silly, David,' said Dot mildly, 'none of us can possibly afford to be anything but forgiving to anyone else, and that includes me. I was just a little upset that you resorted to flippancy once again. Of course we forgive you, however much you exercise our tolerance.'

'I am bound to say,' added Nunc, using that crystal clarity of tone we always associated with him, 'that I have been very much moved and comforted by the way in which this little group of people has accepted and, I hope, loved me, even though I am so different from the rest of you, and not a proper member of your Church of England.'

Dave murmured, 'You're an alien, not a Baptist,' but there was no doubting the pleasure which Nunc's words gave to all of us, especially perhaps to Dot, who had actually comforted our strange little friend when he was at his most vulnerable.

'I forgive Reverend Persimmon and I love Nunc and I would like to hear Mr Craven's poem very much,' said Hartley, summing things up rather neatly.

'Very well,' I responded, as though persuaded against my better judgement, 'but I'll read you something else first, just as a little punishment for our blessed leader here.' I took a sheet of paper from my pocket and smoothed it out on my knee. 'It's been much easier for me to think about Edna's illness and death since the other night, and I've recalled lots of things that I must have pushed to the back of my mind. I suddenly remembered, for instance, something that happened soon after she went into the hospital for – I dunno – the third or fourth time. She was in really bad pain, flat out on the bed, gasping every few seconds as these spasms came, and I was sitting beside her, holding her hand and feeling desperate, when a visitor arrived. It was a chap from her church called Victor Pyford, one of those tall, bony men who always wear ties and need a shave by the middle of the morning. He'd heard that Edna was back in hospital, and thought she might like him to come up and pray for her. Very well-meaning and all that, but you should have heard this prayer of his. Sonorous is not the word! It was mostly about how thankful we should be that we (meaning Edna) were so much better off than some other rather ill-defined section of the community who were suffering much more acutely than we could ever understand. And there was old Eddy, on the point of death virtually, in physical agony, being asked to view her condition as a slight ailment in relative terms.

'I felt quite cross at first, but, as this bloke's funereal voice droned on about how awful everything was, I caught Edna's eye, and we both started to giggle at the same time. She was great like that – marvellous sense of humour even at the worst of times – and I remember thinking then that it would be rather fun to write a slightly exaggerated version of that prayer one day, but I never thought about it again, not until this week, that is.'

Hartley's eyes had been wide with reminiscence and interest as he listened. Now, as he spoke, he seemed to be seeing Edna right in the centre of the flame that burned before us.

'Edna told the old vicar a joke once, and he didn't laugh.'

'The old vicar?' asked Dave.

'The Reverend Stamford-Pargetter, who was here for a long time before you came, Reverend Persimmon. He visited Edna once and asked if she had any questions she wanted to ask. She said there was one, and he looked pleased and asked what it was. She said she wondered if it was true that Anglican clergymen had special check-out counters in supermarkets nowadays, and Reverend Stamford-Pargetter looked very surprised and said. "What on earth do you mean, Miss Craven?" and she said, "Last time I was in the Co-op I could have sworn I saw a sign over one of the counters saying THIRTY-NINE ARTICLES OR LESS." I did not understand the joke, but I did guess that it *was* a joke. Reverend Stamford-Pargetter did not smile at all. He said, "I was not aware of such an innovation, Miss Craven, and I would consider the provision of such a facility extremely unlikely." Then Edna had a little coughing fit, but I think she was laughing really. Later, when the Vicar had gone, she said he was a "clergyman of the cold school", but he would be all right in the end.'

'I think Edna must have said "a clergyman of the *old* school", Hartley dear,' suggested Dot kindly.

'Oh, no, Dot,' I said, 'with all due respect to the Reverend Stamford-Pargetter, I'm quite sure that Hartley has remembered exactly what Edna said. He didn't exactly light any fires, did he? Or do you remember him differently?'

Dot shook her head sadly. 'No,' she admitted, 'he was not a particularly inspiring man, I am afraid.'

'Unlike me, eh, Dot?' said David modestly.

'You have certainly ignited a number of fires, David,' responded Dot with spirit, 'often accidentally, but latterly less indiscriminately.'

'Blimey!' said the Vicar, 'I think we'd better get back to your piece of writing, Dick.'

'Right – well, as I was saying, old Pyford's miserable prayer came back into my mind this week, and it reminded me as well of a wedding I went to a year or so ago. It was one of those very Christian affairs, but quite nice, and it was all going pretty well until the time came for grace to be said before the reception meal began. They'd asked this woman, a female equivalent of Victor Pyford –'

'Needing a shave you mean?' interrupted Dave. I ignored him.

'They'd asked her to say a prayer before we started eating, but it was a big mistake because she was one of those people who are capable of turning the happiest event into something approaching a wake. What the non-Christians thought about it I dread to think.'

I tapped the paper on my knee.

'So, this week, I wrote a highly exaggerated version of what she said, and I only wish old Edna was around to hear it – she'd have laughed her head off. She hated inappropriateness.'

'Come on, then,' said Dave impatiently, cracking his knuckles together, 'let's hear it. I bet it's about as funny as an earwig's digestive tract.'

I held my sheet of paper in both hands and started to read in a thin, cracked voice that rose and fell with monotonous predictability.

This is a joyful occasion, but we would remember those who are covered in great big scabs at this time. We bring before you all crushed persons, and we pray that they may indeed rejoice in their mangled state. Grant peace to gangrene sufferers everywhere, and those who, even now, are about to touch live wires and be burned to a crisp. We hold up before you all roofers whose walkways are not secure; we pray for their limbs, old and new: and we especially recall, as we begin this delicious meal, those frozen folk who are grovelling around in the dark, living on slugs. May they acquire a taste *for* those slugs, and crunch them with joy, even as we shall crunch our prawn starter in a few moments' time.

May we be aware, as we consume this food, that others are *being* consumed, by giant anacondas and hunger-crazed members of the big-cat family who are either too old or too feeble to hunt and catch more appropriate prey.

As these festivities uplift our spirits, let us be one with those who, having been uplifted by sundry aeroplanes, are now forced to vacate them before they land. We thank thee for those who are equipped with parachutes, and we reach out in spirit to those who are not. May they discover that beneath them are the everlasting arms – or a pond.

And so now we pray for this evening, and we ask that food-poisoning and sudden illness will be endured quietly so that the joy of these two young people will be undiminished, both now and at such time as death shall separate them – leaving one an inconsolable widow or widower, and the other a lifeless corpse in the cold ground. AMEN.

And now, let joy be unrestrained . . .

Dave obviously found this piece of nonsense slightly funnier than an earwig's digestive tract. In fact, he laughed so much that his chair toppled over backwards and he performed an ungainly reverse somersault, ending up flat on his stomach gasping for breath. Dot and Hartley were laughing too, but Nunc just smiled and looked at me with a question in his eyes.

'Oh, dear!' groaned the Vicar as he recovered his breath at last. 'I thought I was a goner then, I really did! "Others are being consumed" – oh, dear! That was very funny, Craven, but I have to tell you . . .'

He levered himself off the ground and collapsed back into his chair, which Hartley had just picked up. Rubbing his wet eyes with the back of one large hand, he spoke in a weak little voice.

'Like I said, it was very funny, but I am actually deeply and comprehensively offended by what you've just said. My uncle Rupert was a one-legged roofer, I myself am an absolute slave to gangrene, several of my relatives have been eaten by anacondas, my grandfather on my father's side was known as "Scabs" Persimmon, and I breed slugs as house-pets. I am completely devastated.' A chuckle erupted from deep inside him once again. '"Endured quietly" – oh, dear!'

In the course of Dave's exuberant response our poor little candle had been extinguished, but, if anything, it was lighter than it had been. Nunc glowed brightly as he voiced the thought that he had been silently projecting for the last couple of minutes.

'I pray and beseech you, Richard, to tell us what you have written in verse, even though you are hoping that we shall forget that it exists because you have hidden it behind our laughter.'

Nunc had an extraordinary gift for reshaping and directing events in a particular way. He was absolutely right, of course. I was hoping that we might have parted at this point, leaving the second sheet of paper tucked safely away in my pocket. Now I couldn't avoid reading it. Everyone looked at me with keen anticipation as I produced my further offering.

'It's about death,' I said. 'I haven't wanted even to think about death since Edna died, but this week I remembered how confused I felt on the day when she went. I realized that I'd never properly faced it, not even with her illness pointing that way for so long. Pehaps it was because I hadn't any confidence about what would happen afterwards. And I'm not alone, of course. Death is still treated like some black sheep of the family who returns from exile every now and then, upsetting everybody and disturbing the peace until he clears off again. I want to think about it now. I want to know what it means. So this is just a beginning – an exploration. And the last bit – the last verse – comes out of things that have happened lately, together with what I know Edna believed, so it's really – well, mostly, her saying that part, I suppose.'

I haven't said this to the others who were there that evening, but the next few minutes produced another real turning point for me. I shall never forget those four faces gleaming like orange-tinted moons as I began to read. They were the first people that I really gave myself to. I do pray that there will be others. This is what I read:

What do we do about death?
We don't –
The monster is hidden away.
It's not in the zoo for the public to view
The look on its face would empty the place
We don't want to die, the people would cry
Death is the curse in the back of the hearse
We don't need to see it today.

What do we do about death?
We don't –
We shovel it under the ground
Under the sod and hope there's a God
Whose principles bend at the bitterest end
Or we burn it away, and whispering say
Death is the scream at the end of the dream
There isn't a lonelier sound.

What do we do about death?
We don't –
We don't even give it a name
He's gone before to a distant shore
She's passed away, we gloomily say,
He's fallen asleep in a terminal heap.
Death is the spear that is poisoned with fear
It pierces the heart of the game.

What do we do about death?
We don't –
But once in the angry sun
A winner was slain at the centre of pain
When a battle was fought at the final resort

But because of the cross it was fought without loss
And death is the knife that will free us for life
Because of what Jesus has done.

Part Five

David's Account

David's Account

1

When I read what Dot, Hartley and Dick Craven had written, I laughed like a drain, wept buckets, and got so mad that I bashed the desk with my fist like a sledge-hammer. In fact, you could have stocked a small ironmonger's shop using the responses I came out with that evening. What a pillock! Me, I mean. The awful jokes, the mindless crashing about, the incredible transparency of intention and motivation. I was pleased about some things – all the stuff about Vincent, for instance – but, in the main, I come over like a poorly trained Old English Sheepdog with St Vitus' Dance.

I'm not saying that the Good, the Bad and the Ugly got it wrong. It wouldn't be so bad if they had. The thing that gutted me (to use a theological expression), was the huge gap between how I really am inside and the way I must appear to others. I know that Dot and the others are acquainted with the small, vulnerable, piping little Persimmon who inhabits this yeti of a body, but others must find it very confusing. I was interested to read what my beloved Hartley wrote about losing his voice when people get aggressive. I don't exactly lose my voice, but my spirit becomes emaciated, and I say, or agree with, things that are abhorrent to me. Those who've only met 'Hulk' Persimmon would be amazed.

I remember, for instance, going to a photographer in London to have some pictures done for relatives in

Australia. They'd evinced a masochistic desire to 'see what I looked like now', so I decided to indulge this strange whim.

'Bernie Vallon – Photographer' turned out to be a slightly over-weight slab of a man, dressed in baggy velvet trousers and an unbuttoned silk shirt. His hair was long and lank, framing a wide, well-fed face that was adorned with a permanently sardonic smile. He wore a heavy silver pendant on a leather thong round his neck, and his feet were clad in a pair of yellow wooden clogs that made a horrible clacking noise every time he moved on the lino-covered floor of his studio. I loathed and feared him on sight, and wished I was somewhere else. As he lined up his camera he spoke to me in resonant, streetwise tones, and I shrivelled inwardly.

'I've got a few very special pics of some rather juicy little stackeroos over there,' he said, 'we'll have a drool afterwards.'

I wasn't wearing my collar at the time, so he almost certainly didn't know that I was a clergyman. I doubt if it would have made much difference anyway. He was one of those people who assume that there's mud at the bottom of every human pool. I knew what I wanted to say in response to his grotesque invitation. I'm no less lustful than the next man (sorry – person!) but I truly detest displays of women's bodies for 'drooling' purposes, and even if I didn't, I'm a Christian – of sorts – so I knew exactly what I should have said. But I didn't! Why didn't I? It was something about the confidence and cynical brashness of the man that made my throat close up. The thought of hearing my voice bleating out skinny state-ments about what I believed, was appalling. I felt quite

sure that this fascist of the photography world would take my opinions, my beliefs and my faith, screw them up like a handful of used tissues, and drop them in his pedal-bin.

'Oh really, have you? Well, err . . . see how things go, eh?'

That's what I actually said as I balanced and posed on

the ridiculously tiny stool that he'd sat me on. Things didn't get any better either. In the course of the next twenty minutes I gave my implicit agreement to his proposition that it was reasonable to blow any intruder's head off with an unlicensed shotgun that he kept in the loo by his front door. I squeaked vague assent to his view that all drugs should be freely available to everybody. I produced a slightly unconvinced humming noise when he described white South Africans as profoundly misunderstood in political terms. I silently affirmed his personal conviction that hanging and flogging should be introduced for a range of minor offences that escape my memory at the moment. And I limply lined up with his demand for complete removal of all censorship in every branch of the media, regardless of the age or vulnerability of the recipients.

I emerged from this modern-day Mussolini's King's Cross flat feeling like a moral corpse, loathing him and myself to about the same extent, and apologizing volubly to God in my head, for letting him down so miserably.

I don't want to say much about what happened to me on that evening that Hartley wrote about, except that, in some strange way, I got in touch with the child I used to be, and began to understand for the first time that it was the people making my world fall apart 'on the other side of the door' who took my power to resist away from me. Dominant characters like Bernie Vallon – Photographer, and Nigel Forsyth – Organist, just bring out the crushed kid in me – anyone, in fact, who insists on making me feel the muscles on their opinions.

That's why I was dreading my postponed dinner party with the aforesaid organist. Would it leave me more angry and frustrated than ever, or would some new thing happen to change the situation? I wasn't at all optimistic, but Nunc had said it was a good idea, and, as one of the others said, he seemed to 'know' things, so it was worth a try.

2

'How did your social event go, David?'

That was Dot's first question after we got settled on the Thursday evening after the one when I did a back somersault for the first time in forty years. (I must remember to thank Craven for recording that little indignity so faithfully.) Dick hadn't arrived yet, but the rest of us had decided that the vestry would be a warmer and cosier place to meet than anywhere else on what turned out to be another very stormy night. Dot was seated, despite her protests, in the only armchair in the place, a big shiny leather thing stuffed with something unspeakable. Hartley was enthroned on our first-reserve bishop's chair, I was humbly and sacrificially encased in an ancient, hard, narrow, upright chair beside the desk, and Nunc was perched on the edge of one of those obscure pieces of ecclesiastical furniture that Dick mentioned – always teak and always obsolete. All three bars of the electric fire were working away, and we were lit by a peculiarly ugly standard lamp that I had very generously accepted as a gift from a parishioner who couldn't bring himself to throw it away.

The old church safe was set aside as a punishment for Craven's tardiness if and when he turned up.

'Dot,' I said, 'two weeks ago I hated Nigel Forsyth more

than words could say, but after last night . . .'

'Yes?' encouraged Dot brightly.

'I feel I can express myself quite adequately.'

'Did you garotte Mr Forsyth?' enquired Hartley hopefully.

Dot tutted loudly. 'Are you really saying, David, that nothing has changed at all? I really did believe that you might have been able to move forward in that relationship after what happened here three weeks ago. What is the use of – '

'Hold on, Dot!' I held my hands up in surrender. 'You don't quite understand. Spending an evening with dear Nigel only confirmed my view – confirmation's always welcome to us Anglicans – that he is a rat of the first order. The difference is that I have a bit more grip nowadays on the fact that I am just a rat of another species. Also, we were trained in completely different mazes by two completely different sets of lab technicians, so it's not really surprising that we're err . . . completely different.'

'Never mind the lecture on determinism, David,' said Dot, with the acerbity that I adore in her, 'what *really* made the difference?'

I sighed and squirmed in my wooden trap. 'I was vulnerable, Dot. I've only tried it with you lot before, but I decided to try it with Nigel last night and see what happened.'

'You usually go quiet when you speak to Mr Forsyth, don't you, Reverend Persimmon.' It was a perfectly innocent comment from Hartley.

'Yes, Hartley,' I replied, 'you're absolutely right. I do usually go quiet when I speak to Mr Forsyth, but it wasn't quite the same this time because I started off by trying to be as honest as I could and as weak as I really felt. And,' I added, glancing sideways at Dot, 'I did not, on this occasion, attempt to fuel my courage with any little snifters before the meal. I prayed instead, although I'm not sure how the creator of the universe felt about being an alternative to a treble scotch.'

'What is a treble scotch, David?' asked Nunc quietly from his perch.

'It is a large, strong drink,' said Dot, 'that makes your head spin and your legs tremble. It produces a quite spurious sensation of confidence and competence, and is best avoided on the whole.'

'I believe that the creator of the universe has taken quite humble forms himself,' murmured Nunc with a smile.

'Well,' I continued, 'leaving aside the intriguing question of how Dot comes to be such an expert on the effects of strong drink – I started by explaining to Nigel why I'd asked him round.'

'Because you do not like him, you mean?' queried Hartley.

'I wasn't quite as tactless as that, Hartley, surprising as that might seem, but I was pretty straight. Dick was in the kitchen putting the finishing touches to our prussic acid starter, so Nigel and I sat down with our elegant little sherries in the sitting room, and the conversation went more or less as follows.

Me: I expect you're wondering why I asked you round tonight?

Nigel: Not at all, unless it's your policy to invite people to dinner once every three years instead of visiting them regularly.

Me: (*Wanting to kill him and feeling all my confidence
            drain away at the same time*) Do you mean that
            you're upset about me not visiting you since I
            came to St Wilfred's, Nigel?

Nigel: (*Somewhat taken aback*) Well, no, not really – not
            upset exactly, just a little surprised.

Me: Well, will you forgive me for not visiting you?
            You're quite right – I should have visited you, but
            I felt such a failure in our relationship that I wasn't
            able to face it. That's one of the reasons I asked
            you to dinner. I wanted to see if I could make
            things any better between us. We haven't been
            able to agree on much, have we? You always make
            me feel small and silly – I don't mean you're to
            blame for that. All that started long before we ever
            met. But we don't get on, do we?

Nigel: (*Speechless for a few moments, and unusually ill at
            ease*) I'm not sure what you're getting at exactly,
            but if you mean that I'm not happy with the way
            you've approached some aspects of work in this
            parish – then, yes, you're right. Ronald Stamford-
            Pargetter, your predecessor, had a very strong
            musical and sacramental sense, and I have been
            disappointed that the tradition he established
            hasn't been maintained. As far as our personal
            relationship is concerned – well, I think we are
            very different kinds of people. You, if you don't
            mind me saying so, seem to agree with everything
            I say or suggest when we're actually speaking, and
            subsequently fail to put into practice anything that
            I thought was settled.

Me: That's something else I'd like you to forgive me

for. I've been very weak and unassertive. And I've said things about you – very unloving things – behind your back. You'll have to forgive me for that as well.

Nigel: I really don't think –

Me: Oh, and I forgive *you* for what you said about *me*.

Nigel: I can assure you that I'm not in the habit of gossiping to anybody about the Vicar – unless you can recall something specific. Perhaps, being a student of scripture, you're able to quote chapter and verse.

Me: I was thinking of what you said to Stanley in the choir about me coming to St Wilfred's. About the Old Testament verse that prophesied my arrival. Jonah, chapter four, verse seven, I think it was – 'The Lord appointed a worm.' Remember? I was really upset and angry when I heard that, Nigel, but over the last couple of weeks, as I said, I realized how many negative things I've said about you. So let's forgive each other, eh?

Nigel: (*A strange purple colour*) I certainly don't regard comments made in privacy to close personal friends as gossip or public criticism. And, to be absolutely frank, I find all this talk of mutual forgiveness rather repellent. We are two grown men placed by random circumstances in a situation where we are obliged to work together. I am the church organist, and you are the priest in charge of St Wilfred's. That may need some adjustment of roles, but I refuse to indulge in pointless sentimentalism. If you don't mind me saying so, Reverend Presimmon, it's just this kind of immature approach to problems that has created so many tensions in the church of late. In any case, Stanley should never have repeated what I said.

Me: Did you only say it to him then, Nigel? (*Silence*) I know I'm rather immature. I either shout or bleat. I know I've got a lot of things wrong, but we've all got faults, haven't we? (*Silence*) You have a particular talent for music – you're a superb organist [Oh, the *pain*!] and I'm not superb at anything, but I do want to follow Jesus now. We've got that in common, haven't we?

Nigel: (*Shaking his head*) What I have is a respect for the Church and its traditions, and I don't think we have that in common, if you don't mind me saying so . . .

And then Dick came in and said the meal was ready, and Nigel brightened up. He's quite keen on Dick because he's a real writer, and very good company and all that. I didn't say very much more – went on being as nice as I could to the phantom of the oratorio, but he obviously found me about as interesting as a second-hand breadboard.'

'I am come that they might have some adjustment of roles, and have it in moderation,' misquoted Nunc softly. 'How did it make you feel, David?'

'Oddly enough,' I said, 'I felt unusually free . . .'

At that precise moment my chair 'burst', just as Craven came in through the door. I have never seen Hartley laugh with such total abandonment. He didn't quite do my back somersault trick – his throne was too solid for that – but he did literally cry with laughter, hanging limply over to one side like a bonfire-night guy. I tried to look dignified, but failed as usual.

'S-s-so funny!' wheezed Hartley, 'just as you s-s-said about being f-f-free, your chair went b-b-bang! So f-f-funny!'

'Have I missed the cabaret, Dave?' Dick smiled at Hartley's helpless mirth. 'I'm sorry I'm late, but I've just had your bosom buddy on the phone. Nigel seems more than a bit puzzled about last night. Where do I sit, by the way?' I pointed at the safe. 'You're sure you haven't rigged it up with a dynamite charge, Dave? I know you like to keep us all laughing if you can.'

'I've just been talking about last night,' I said, picking up pieces of side-of-chair as I spoke. 'I was just saying that, although I didn't get anywhere at all with Forsyth yesterday evening, I felt quite calm and relaxed. Mind you, if he'd said "if you don't mind me saying so" once or twice more, I might have gone for his throat. He didn't budge an inch.'

'I thought you did well, Dave,' said Craven, planting himself on top of the safe. 'Couple of little barbs tucked away among the peace moves, but, on the whole, very impressive. Mind you, I had to do most of the talking for the rest of the evening, but I didn't mind that – in fact, I thought I was rather brilliant.'

Hartley had recovered at last. 'Please forgive me, Reverend Persimmon,' he said, 'I seem to laugh at you a great deal nowadays, but I promise you it is only because you look so funny.'

'Oh, that's all right, then,' I replied, a little drily, 'as long as it's only because I look so funny. Anyway – to summarize, Nigel Forsyth and I are not about to announce our imminent engagement, but on the other hand, I'm not as worried or threatened by him today as I was yesterday. And . . .' I paused, slightly embarrassed.

'And what?' asked Dot.

'And I've started to pray for him – among others, of course. In fact I've only just started praying again since that business three weeks ago, and it has made a difference. It's like – I dunno – massaging reality.'

'How did that come about, David?' Dot wanted to know. 'You have not told us anything of events following that evening. Did anything significant happen?'

I moved uneasily on my sideless chair.

'Well, I suppose something did happen, but . . . I wasn't really planning to tell anyone about it. I *will* tell you – if you want me to, but I don't want anybody to laugh, or I shall stop talking and sing several songs. It's all right, Hartley' – the poor chap's face had turned slightly pale – 'I know that if *you* laugh it's only because I look so funny.'

Craven of the Lower Fifth raised a hand tentatively.

'Yes, Craven,' I responded, 'sit up straight, lad, and speak clearly. Stop dribbling and don't annoy the others.'

'I was just wondering if it was all right to be extremely amused on a profound level, but without showing it. Is it? Oh, and here's a joke. Why am I like a Conservative election candidate in Tunbridge Wells?' He tapped the metal beneath him. 'Because I've got a safe seat.'

'There you are,' I said, indicating the absence of any amusement on the faces of Dot and Hartley. 'Their reaction to your appalling joke is precisely what I expect as my moving narrative unfolds. Do I make myself quite clear?'

'Please tell us what happened, David,' said Dot

patiently. 'All this absurdity shows me quite clearly that something did happen, and that it meant a great deal to you. I, for one, will not laugh, as you very well know. You are simply causing deliberate delay and Richard is not helping.'

'Were you confused on that Friday morning, David?'

Nunc's gentle question had its usual unlocking effect.

'I was confused, Nunc, yes. I wasn't expecting God to drop in for coffee like Craven, but I wanted something to happen. All the stuff about meeting that poor little kid I used to be was necessary, but more than anything else it had a sort of rubbish-clearing effect. It left me sitting at my desk on the Friday morning, looking more or less squarely at the person I was, underneath all the blustering and criticism of others, and it was not a pretty sight. I picked up my Bible and tried to read a few verses, but I couldn't settle to it. I tried to feel sorry for myself, but I couldn't get it together as well as I usually do. Last of all, I took refuge in calories – '

'Oh David!' remonstrated Dot.

'But even six slices of toast, butter and marmalade didn't seem to bring me any closer to God.'

'Seven might have done it,' said Dick, 'with coffee.'

'So I stomped back to my desk, caught my finger in the rolltop when it rolled shut, swore loudly – '

'Oh, David!'

'Apologized to the Cloud of Witnesses, who were probably all having a jolly good laugh at my expense, and suddenly found that my tongue was untied and I really wanted to talk to God. When I say that, I don't mean that I wanted to do something religious – I mean, quite simply, that I wanted to talk – to sound off – at God, so I did. The funny thing was . . .'

I paused for a moment, a bit embarrassed again, and looked round at the others.

'Did God speak to you, David?' asked Nunc.

'Well, you lot tell me first if he's ever spoken to you.'

'No,' said Hartley cheerfully, 'he has not spoken to me – not as far as I know anyway. He used to speak to Edna, though, and sometimes it was about me. Then she would tell me what he had said.'

'What about you, Dot?'

'He speaks to me,' said Dot slowly, 'through the Bible, and the natural world, and the words of others. And sometimes,' she looked at Nunc, 'through pictures in my mind, or even words that just enter my thoughts unexpectedly. He is after all a bespoke God, not an off-the-peg one. He will speak as he wishes.'

'Craven?'

'Yes, we do the crossword together on a Friday evening and – sorry, Dave, felt a bit self-conscious. I guess I'm ready to believe he can do anything he wants really. Edna certainly reckoned he spoke directly to her sometimes, but I'm not sure what she meant. He certainly spoke to me here two weeks ago, but I think that was sort of special – not a Monday morning communication, if you know what I mean. I'm babbling. I don't know what I think.'

'I talk to God in a funny language sometimes,' said Hartley.

Silence.

'What do you mean by that, Hartley?' asked Dot. 'Who told you to do it?'

'Nobody told me to do it,' answered Hartley evenly. 'I was walking down by the river one day, looking for frogs, and suddenly a funny language bubbled up inside me and out of my mouth. I thought it was to do with God, but I was not sure, so I asked Edna – '

'You're talking about years ago?'

'Yes, Reverend Persimmon, it was about a month before Edna died. I asked her what it was and – ' Hartley went slightly pink, 'she kissed me and said it was a present from God to make it easier to talk to him when I didn't know what to say. And it *has* been – I mean it is. I like it very much.'

'You never told me about this, Hartley,' I said, still rather dazed.

'Nor me,' added Dot. 'Why did you not mention it to David or me?'

'Nobody asked me,' said Hartley simply, 'and I did not think it had anything to do with the church. Has it anything to do with the church?'

'Hartley,' I decided to explain his experience to him, 'this funny language you talk about is actually – '

'A present from God to make it easier to talk to him when Hartley doesn't know what to say.' Nunc's clear voice completed my sentence with irresistible authority. 'Did God speak to you, David?'

Obviously, any further discussion of Hartley's funny language was not to be allowed. Why did we accept Nunc's decisions so readily on these occasions? Don't ask me – we just did.

'Well, I think he spoke to me, but not – you know – not through a public-address system or anything like that.'

I stood up, wanting to pace for a moment, but there was no room to move, so I sat down again, rather annoyed. An ounce more intelligence would have suggested that a chair

whose sides were so easily demolished was unlikely to withstand the high velocity downward impact of eighteen stone of angry clergyman. I went straight through the damn thing, giving myself a bruised backside, and the assembled company yet another excuse to laugh their socks off. Craven helped me up as if I was an advanced geriatric, and led me to his cast-iron safe, saying, 'Now, don't sit down too hard this time, there's a good gentleman.'

'When you've all finished cackling about the damage to my bottom, pehaps I can tell you about my divine experience. Are you all right on the floor, Dick?' He nodded. 'Good! Why are you turning purple, Hartley? Go on, let it out for goodness' sake!'

At last, even Hartley's explosive mirth had subsided, and I was able to go on.

'It wasn't so much God talking to me as a sort of dialogue that I pursued in my mind. Do I sound like a loony, or does that mean anything to anyone else?'

Dot nodded vigorously, Hartley shook his head vigorously, Nunc smiled encouragingly, and Craven mouthed the word 'loony'.

'Well, whatever it was, it made a difference, and I'm going to tell you about it. "God," I said, "I feel rotten in every way, not just physically, but in all ways. Thanks for what happened in the church yesterday, but all it seems to have done is show me how grotty I am. I feel about as interesting as the contents of someone else's winning rummy hand. You could measure most of my moods with a seismograph. My body feels like one of those old-fashioned diving suits, only less comfortable and more heavily weighted. Come on God!" I pleaded, "what about a spot of divine intervention? Bring about some nice miraculous change in my miserable condition".'

'And did he do a miracle?' asked Hartley excitedly.

'Well, this is where the old dialogue got started, you see – if that's what it was. He said, "I don't know about miracles, but you're already aware of seven practical areas that need a lot more effort and attention than you've been giving them."

'"Practical areas?" I repeated warily. "Actually I was rather hoping for a mir – "

'"Yes, practical areas. I'll go through them for you, shall I?"

'"Go on then," I muttered ungraciously, "away you go."

'"Right," he said, "let's start with the whole area of routine. You're very disorganized, David. You've got to give yourself a clear context to operate in. Why not take the dog for a walk at the same time each morning? Start work at a fixed time and make sure a reasonable breakfast gets fitted in *before* you begin. Last week your sermon was covered with marmalade. What about being really revolutionary and dealing with the post on the same day that it arrives? Could you bear to leave the phone off the hook? Or get an answerphone? I don't know! I spend half my time getting the over-organized types out of their strangling routines, and the other half rescuing people like you from total chaos.

'"Then we come to diet. You notice I said a *reasonable* breakfast. You assume I'm only interested in spiritual abstracts, but I am also concerned about your gut, dear son of mine. There is too much of it. It protrudes. You are becoming positively pre-natal. Do I make myself clear?"

"'Yes, but – "

"'Seriously, David, how can you honestly expect to operate properly when you're this overweight? Get hold of a sensible diet – again – and I might be able to offer a sprinkling of miracle dust when you reach breaking point. You'll be amazed at the improvement in all areas once you're down to par. I made the kit – I know!"

"'Yes, but – "

"'Let's move on to the subject of alcohol.'"

"'Ah, but – "

"'The history of your liver reads like one of those *Build Up To War* textbooks. You've had hepatitis twice, and there was a period in your life when you seemed intent on embalming yourself. I know the days of those wild binges are gone, and, as always, you have perfect freedom in this matter. I've nothing against alcohol as such; all I'm saying is that you'd better watch it!'"

"'Yes, but – "

"'Fourthly, we come to the little matter of rest. You children of the sixties are all the same – terrified of going to bed at a reasonable time in case something exciting happens at one o'clock in the morning. Some people can do it, David – Mrs Thatcher can do it. You can't! You'd be amazed how many so-called spiritual problems are caused by over-tiredness. Besides, you're not as young as you used to be.'"

"'I wonder if I could just – "

"'And now, David, let's face it, the thing you're most lacking is any form of exercise. Your blood pressure is the only part of you that moves quickly. You used to enjoy tennis and badminton and cricket. Now it takes a block and tackle to get you out of your armchair. Don't worry!

When the diet and the rest and the routine get going you'll be back to Daley Thompson mode in no time."

"'I wouldn't mind – "

"'Talking about routine, we must meet regularly. I know you hiss, shout, moan and plead with me from time to time, and I don't mind – I can handle it. But the kind of person you are needs to be fuelled for each day by a chunk of solid contact with me. Not that it's any hardship, as you well know. Whenever we have met properly like that the experience has brought you a lot of peace, a commodity which, I happen to know, has been at the top of every gift-list you've ever written. Be your own Father Christmas. Fit me into your routine and I'll guarantee to be there, even if you get cross with me – again."

"'Finally, there's Bible-reading."

"'Perhaps I should – "

"'Do *read* the Bible. Don't nibble at it like a nervous mouse with the cat's cheese. Read a chapter – or a book. Get an idea of the sweep of the thing. If there's anything you specially need to notice I'll make sure you don't miss it. Ask me what things mean. Talk to me about it. It's my book. I've sold more copies than Jeffrey Archer, and in a lot more languages."

"'And that concludes my seven-point plan for you, David Persimmon. Away you go!'"

'Which all goes to show, I suppose,' said Craven, from his place on the floor at Dot's feet, 'that if you don't want any answers from God you shouldn't ask him any questions. Your part of the dialogue was very impressive, Dave. You almost completed a sentence once or twice.'

'Do you think there was a bit of God in that, Dot?' I asked, 'or do you think I was just talking to myself and being hopeful? Now that I say it again it sounds a bit practical – ordinary.'

Dot smiled sweetly. 'I am a very stupid old lady in many ways, but in my slow and painful journeys towards the realization that I know nothing, I have at least come to understand a little about the divine ordinariness of God. The thing is, David – ' Dot's smile didn't fade at all as tears filled her eyes ' – every encounter with God that I've ever experienced, every *real* one, has been like waking up from a nightmare. It feels like coming back to what is real and warm and familiar. I think God is very practical, and I think he fits into his own world very easily and very naturally. He became very ordinary for us, didn't he?'

We sat in silence for a little while, thinking about what Dot had said. Then Nunc spoke to me.

'David, which member of your founder's first group of followers do you feel closest to?'

'Peter,' I answered without hesitation, 'although I'm not sure that he and I are the same. I guess Jesus is saying to me, "You are Persimmon, and upon this blancmange I shall build a short phase in the life of this small part of my Church." But – yes, definitely, it would be Peter.'

'I have read,' said Nunc, 'how this Peter leaped from his fishing boat and ran through the water when he saw his master on the shore. He did not understand at that time why his master had lived or died or come back to life again, did he?'

'He did not', I agreed.

'And he had no understanding or knowledge of what the future might hold for him or his companions. Is that not true?'

I nodded.

'Was it not also the case that his three denials had not yet been discussed between himself and the one that he denied?'

'It *was* the case, Nunc. There was unfinished business between them.'

'Why, then, did he run with such abandon towards his master on that day, do you suppose?'

For several seconds Nunc's question seemed to hang in the air between us, something fragile and essential, as Dick put it afterwards. Hartley and I answered with exactly the same words at exactly the same time.

'Because he loved him.'

'And what was this man whom he loved?'

'He was the son of God,' said Dot.

'He was the saviour of mankind,' said Dick.

'He was the one who made everything,' said Hartley.

Nunc shone like Christmas as he asked his next question.

'And this son of God, this saviour of mankind, this one who made everything – what was he doing when Peter arrived, breathless and dripping wet, on the shore? What solemn and majestic task was Peter's risen Lord engaged in?'

My voice broke just a little as I replied.

'He was cooking breakfast for his friends.'

'Is that ordinary and practical enough for you, Dave?' queried my friend from the floor. 'Thank goodness God's not like Cecil B. De Mille, eh?'

'Do you think it's still like that, Nunc?' I said, passionately wanting it to be so.

'I am only an alien,' said Nunc, 'and you are the ones he came to in the form of a man because he loved you, but it seems to me that he still waits quietly on the shore of the real world, still willing to feed those who love him, to settle and forgive the sins with which they have hurt him, and to send them out with quiet minds and stronger hearts to bring others to him.'

3

For a matter of minutes after this speech of Nunc's we sat in one of the most relaxed and companionable silences I've ever known – quite amazing for me. I *hate* silences. But this one – well, it was different. It was broken eventually by Hartley, who stared at me with frowning concentration as he spoke.

'How are you going to stop saying horrible things about Mr Forsyth from now on, Reverend Persimmon? Because you do say horrible things when he's not here, don't you? And if you want to do what the Bible says – '

I clapped my hand to my head. 'All right, Hartley! I've got the message, old chap. I do want to do what the Bible says – in fact it was only yesterday that I suddenly realized what Nunc meant when he said that I'd know what he eats because it was Jesus' favourite food.'

'Something to do with the Samaritan woman at the well, didn't he say?'

'That's right, Dick. I looked it up. It was after Jesus sent all the disciples off to whatever the Samaritan equivalent of Tesco's was to get food. I don't know why he sent *all* of 'em – needed a break from the fuss and prattle probably. Then, when they came back, he said he didn't need the stuff they'd brought because he'd got food of his own.'

Dot quoted confidently. '"My food is to obey the will of the one who sent me, and to finish the work he gave me to do." That is what Nunc was referring to.'

'Precisely, Dot, and I'd like to be fed that too. I don't think I could push a plate of steak and onions away if obedience was the only other thing on the menu, but I have got the point, and next Sunday morning – ' I reached across to one of the smaller items of ecclesiastical furniture and took some papers from a shallow drawer ' – I shall be delivering this sermon – ' I waved my papers ' – to the congregation as a whole, but mainly to myself. As those of you who attend church *every* Sunday know (you may well scratch your ear, Craven), I have been speaking on the commandments. This Sunday coming would have been number ten, which is, of course, the one that deals with covetousness, but because I used one Sunday for my public entrail display, it's actually, and perhaps providentially, number nine.'

'Which is, of course – '

'Exactly, Dot, perfect, eh?'

'David, may I ask you to do something for me?' Nunc's voice was strangely little and lacking in confidence suddenly. He seemed even smaller than usual. 'Would you very much mind delivering your sermon now, this evening?'

'I'm not averse to inflicting pain on my friends, Nunc, but why? Do you really want to end up hearing it twice?'

Nunc's whiteness grew so pale that he actually seemed less visible.

'I shall not hear it twice,' he whispered.

It was like a shock-wave passing through the air of the vestry. Hartley didn't quite catch on, but Dot and Craven and I did. We all started speaking at once.

'Are you saying – '

'Do you mean that – '

'But why should – '

'I will explain afterwards,' said Nunc, his quiet tones cutting short our questioning as effectively as ever.

'Do you really want me to read this stuff?' I asked uncertainly.

Nunc nodded, and there didn't seem to be anything else to do really – except begin. So, after glancing round at my strange little congregation, I began.

I'm always hoping to discover some law or commandment in the Bible that I haven't broken. To date, I have been singularly unsuccessful. By the definitions that Jesus used I have to confess that, at one time or another, I have broken every single one of the ten commandments.

I wish there was something in Exodus about not drinking caustic soda, for instance, because I can honestly say that I have never done such a thing. Oh, for a verse that says: 'Inward and outward shalt thou breathe, outward and inward both, by turns, breathe thou shalt, else thou shalt die, saith the Lord.' I've always been *very* strict indeed about that; but will I get any credit for my steadfast attention to this duty? Of course I won't, because it's not in the book. God is so very selective!

This morning we focus on the ninth commandment, as it is written in the book of Exodus, chapter twenty, verse sixteen. Over the past couple of months we've mopped up the previous eight, so perhaps we can assume that nobody here has a problem any longer with worshipping the wrong god, making false images, using God's name for evil purposes, failing to observe the sabbath, lacking respect for parents, committing murder, committing adultery or committing theft. If you've been casting an envious eye on your neighbour's wives or donkeys, I'm afraid you'll have to wait until next week when we do number ten.

Incidentally, if you missed one, there's no problem at all. They've all been taped. If you've committed adultery, for instance, just come and tell me you need to hear the sermon on adultery and I'll lend you the tape. Furthermore, I'll be able to share your problem with a few people in confidence and just for prayer, which very neatly brings us to this morning's subject.

The ninth commandment: Do not accuse anyone falsely. Or, in its broadest sense: Do not say anything about another person that is not true.

'Well,' you may be wanting to ask, 'do you, David Persimmon, our saintly incumbent, ever say things about other people that are not true?' After carefully considering the question for several seconds, I realized that the answer was – Yes, I do. Exodus, chapter twenty-three, verse one restates this ninth commandment of ours in a form that sums up the way in which I and others tend to fail: Do not spread false rumours. Not that it's much less damaging if they're true.

I've had trouble with this all my life, and I guess that those of us with an ego-strength equivalent to watered down Watney's are always going to be tempted in this area. I'm well aware that we Christians claim that bit in the seventh chapter of Romans (I don't do what I want to do – I do what I don't want to do, and all that) like the Yanks claim the fifth amendment, but it's true. I *don't* want to speak negatively about other people, and I do realize that when I do, dear fellow-ratbags, my motivation is usually defensive. Know what I mean? Damaging someone else's reputation in the course of conversation has the effect of buoying up my self-image. They decrease, and I, as it were, increase. Pathetic, eh?

Mind you, it's also true that I don't tell outrageously extravagant untruths about people. I don't tell everybody that Stanley Carstairs is a K.G.B. agent, or that Richard Craven models fish-net tights in his spare time. It's much more subtle than that, and more difficult to control. For a while I tried to avoid the gossip trap by countering every negative remark made by someone else with a positive one. This can have rather a deadening effect on conversations that were supposed to move smoothly into a time of cosy criticism, but it certainly does the trick. And it's needed.

When I first came to St Wilfred's I remember hearing two comments about two separate people. One person said, of a lady in the church: 'She's the bitterest woman I've ever known.'

Another equally charitable communicant pointed out a fellow Anglican and whispered darkly: 'You want to be careful with that one.'

In both cases my opinion of these two blackguards

was coloured and distorted before I had a chance to find out anything about them for myself. Not only that, but both pieces of gratuitous information turned out to be quite inaccurate. The woman was horribly unhappy, but certainly not bitter, and as for the man – well, I'm still waiting to find out what I've got to be careful of.

But I can't judge, because I do it too.

It's very easy, if we've seen the less attractive side of somebody for three and a half minutes on a Monday morning, to assume that they must be like that for the other six days, twenty-three hours, fifty-six minutes and thirty seconds of the week, and to pass on our juicy but limited knowledge to someone else.

And it doesn't even have to involve words, as we all know. There is that familiar scenario where I say with cheerful innocence: 'We've been getting to know George – he's a great bloke, isn't he?'

The person I've spoken to doesn't reply in words at all, but what eloquence there is in the meaningful silence, the raised eyebrows, the studied avoidance of any normal response.

'The things I could tell you!' all this body language seems to say, 'if I was the sort of person who criticizes others behind their backs, which I'm not, as you can see.'

As I said, I have tried to fight negative with positive in the past, but I haven't done too well lately. Every now and then I find myself slipping into what I call the 'just between the twenty-nine of us' trap, more subtle and even more deadly than the jolly old body language.

The most likely setting to this phenomenon is an evening meal with friends. We're well into the main course, the wine is trickling steadily – if not flowing – and the conversation proceeds as follows.

'I want you to tell me what you think about something,' says one of my guests in an adult, let's-get-down-to-brass-tacks sort of tone.

'Yes?' say I, thrilled as ever to grace the world with my opinion.

'How do you think the new Methodist minister's coping with the job?'

Roughly translated this means: 'Let's rubbish Henry Harper, the new Methodist bloke.'

'I've got a lot of time for Henry,' I reply, letting my face express a mixture of mature concern and willingness to collude.

'Oh, me too,' enthuses my guest, recognizing quite rightly that until we've established how honourable our intentions are, we can't comfortably proceed with the criticism.

'Why do you ask?' I enquire, mentally snuggling into the gossip bed.

'Well,' says the guest, 'look – can I say something that won't go beyond these four walls?'

This is the afore mentioned 'just between the twenty-nine of us' trap, and now, of course, I'm on the edge of my seat. He's going to say something horrible about Henry – great!

'Well,' he continues, 'Henry's great with the kids in his church.'

'Wonderful!' I agree.

'And he's got a real talent for organization.'

'Absolutely!'

'It's just – '

My guest pauses, his brow furrowed, his face contorted, as though the words he is about to say are produced at enormous personal cost.

'Frankly, I sometimes wonder if old Henry is a Christian at all!'

I nod sagely.

'Not,' he continues earnestly, 'that I'm talking behind his back – I'd say it to his face.'

'Of course!' I nod vigorously, knowing that only by colluding in this outrageous lie can we continue satisfactorily with our interesting discussion about this trivial little deficiency in Henry's ministry.

After an evening like the one I've just described, I usually feel shabby and ashamed. It's a sort of moral hangover, I suppose. Like someone who gets blind drunk on a Friday night, I spend most of the next day vowing that I will never, ever do it again. But when the temptation comes along once more, it's just as alluring and just as difficult to resist. The tongue, as James points out, is probably the most dangerous part of the body. So easy to use it to produce words that can never be taken back again.

I remember a friend telling me how she sat in a pub with a work colleague, making exaggerated complaints about the child-care shift that had been on duty before hers the previous day.

'It's absolutely typical of Ted's shift,' she said, 'that the place was left in a disgusting, untidy mess, and the kids all in filthy moods. It makes me sick!'

'Actually,' said her companion, 'it wasn't Ted's

shift – it was mine.'

'Oh,' said my friend lamely, her face reddening, 'well, it wasn't that bad really . . .'

Criticism among Christians is deadly. Gossip and backbiting can be the cause of great wounds in the body of Christ, and they'll almost certainly involve hypocrisy and judgementalism, which are just as bad for the doers as for the receivers.

As for accurate accusation – well, obviously it has its place, but it can be just as damaging, especially when it hasn't allowed for the possibility of change.

'I worked with him thirty years ago and I know what he's like. Wouldn't trust him farther than I could throw him . . .'

People do change – even I might be changing a bit. Are you going to let me be different? Am I going to let you be different? I know I've either exploded or run away in the past. Will you let me change? Will you *help* me to change, if God helps as well?

I sometimes wonder about the servant girl who heard Peter deny Jesus three times. Did she pass that juicy little anecdote around over the next few years as Peter became more and more famous?

'If you only knew,' she might have said, 'what I know about that man. If you'd seen and heard what I did, you wouldn't think he was so wonderful.'

Was she there when he was crucified upside down out of deference to the man he had once betrayed? I bet that closed her mouth. And perhaps that's the proper response to the challenge of this awkward ninth commandment. I'm asking God every day to help me keep my mouth shut unless I've got something good or useful to say. I've failed from time to time, but I'm still praying and I'm still trying. Won't you join me? Amen.

4

I felt a bit self-conscious in the pause that followed this piece of glorious sermonizing, but the response was quite good really. Nunc nodded, and said, still in a very small voice, 'Yes, we must love each other, that is the most important and the most difficult thing.'

Dot said, 'Bravo, David, we really need that kind of sermon just as much as the other sort.'

People have always said that sort of thing about my sermons. The other kind of sermon is, presumably, the learned, profound, expository sort of message. Great, if you can do it, but I can't.

'Good stuff, Dave,' said Dick, 'the only thing is – you and I are going to have to think of something else to talk about when we go out to dinner, aren't we? Good thing, probably. Edna would think so for sure.'

'What did Nunc mean when he said that he would not hear Reverend Persimmon's sermon twice?'

Hartley had probably been chewing the question over throughout my peroration. Now that the implication of Nunc's statement was beginning to become clear to him he looked deeply troubled. And so were the rest of us troubled. It was Craven who put it into words for us.

'Are you leaving us, Nunc – is that what you meant?'

'I am called home,' said Nunc, his voice faint with sorrow and something else. 'If I do not go I shall starve . . .'

Once again, Craven and Dot and I all started talking at once. Then, one by one, we dried up and looked at Hartley in his bishop's chair. He wasn't making any sound at all, just sitting very straight with his hands pressed flat against his eyes, as though he believed that if he held the tears in, the sorrow might stay inside as well. He spoke from behind his hands.

'I do not want you to go, Nunc. Please stay.'

'I cannot stay,' said Nunc, 'but I will see you all again. I will see you, Dot, and you will be very happy. I will see you, Richard, and you will have become sure. I will see you, David, and you will be at peace with yourself.'

He slipped off his seat and placed a gentle hand on Hartley's shoulder. Hartley took his hands away from his face and looked at his small friend. His poor old face was a picture of misery.

'Hartley,' said Nunc, 'I wish you could come with me, but you cannot. I will see you again, though, and you will be almost exactly the same as you are now.'

He left his hand on Hartley's shoulder for a moment before addressing us as a group.

'I wonder if you would all be so kind as to come with me to a right place for saying farewell.'

'We will go anywhere you wish, Nunc,' said Dot, her voice catching a little. 'It seems so sudden . . .'

'Okay, Nunc,' said Craven, pretending to be cool and practical, 'where d'you want us to go?' He stood up and brushed himself down.

I stood up as well, wondering what the 'right' place would turn out to be. I was suddenly terribly afraid of the cold.

'The top of the tower,' said Nunc, 'may we go to the top

of the tower? That is a right place for goodbyes.'

Dick and I looked at each other. I knew we were both thinking the same thing. Dot hadn't a snowball's chance in Church House of ever getting to the top of the tower because of her arthritis. Dot obviously realized it as well.

'Nunc dear,' she said, 'you and I must say goodbye here, then the others will go with you to the tower. I am afraid that my silly old joints simply won't carry me up all those steps.'

Nunc looked genuinely puzzled.

'But it is the *right* place,' he said, with an emphasis that I didn't comprehend at all. Dot didn't understand either.

'I would love to do as you ask,' she protested, almost tearfully, 'but I have arthritis. I cannot climb those steps, Nunc!'

'But David is here,' replied Nunc, 'and you have been a Bible-basher for fifty years, Dot. And,' he repeated, 'it is the *right* place.'

Dot suddenly clicked. She turned to face me, her eyes alight with hope. 'David,' she said, 'please pray for my healing – now – please . . .'

I hope there isn't a special hell for facetious vicars. Not that I felt facetious. I felt scared and totally lacking in faith. I had never in my life actually laid hands on anyone for healing, and, although I believed God could heal in a general sense, I'd never seen it happen for myself. I'm sure I went white.

'We only have healing services when there's a ninth Sunday in the month.'

Those were the words that squeaked out of my mouth. But Dot wasn't having any of it.

'David Persimmon,' she rapped imperiously, 'I am

going to the top of that tower, and you are going to co-operate with God in making it possible. Hartley, get off that chair and let me sit down. Thank you very much. Right! I'm ready.'

'Come on, Dave,' said Dick, 'we'll all put our hands on her and you pray.'

As we gathered around Dot's seated figure I was conscious of two things. First, Nunc was doing his nightlight impression. That gave me a bit of confidence. Then, as I looked at Dick's face I saw some sort of battle being fought out behind his eyes, and I realized how hard it must be for him to truly desire healing for Dot when his sister had never found relief from suffering. Hartley was muttering something to himself very quietly as he stood behind Dot's chair, eyes closed, hand resting lightly on her back. I swallowed hard, put both hands on Dot's head, and made some words come out of my mouth.

'Father God, we all love Dot.' I stopped, straining to make sure that everything I said was true. 'You love her as well. We'd all like her to be healed of this horrible arthritis, and we believe you want it more than we do. So – well, why not? In the name of Jesus, we ask for the arthritis to disappear. We haven't got much faith – at least, I haven't – so we need a boost for what we have got. Please make her well again, for Jesus' sake, amen.'

We stayed where we were for a little while, then drew back and looked at Dot. She opened her eyes very wide and smiled serenely.

'Well,' she said, 'are we going up this tower or aren't we?'

'Are you better?' asked Hartley, voicing the question we all wanted to ask.

'I'll tell you in a minute,' answered Dot. 'Come on everybody, we had better start our climb . . .'

Up on top of the tower the weather was frenzied. Great gusts of wind blew a stinging spray of fine rain into our faces as we gathered together on the flat roof and linked arms to form a circle. Above us, black clouds glowered heavily, disappointed that we should so willingly defy the storm. I shone the flash-lamp I'd brought from the vestry onto the faces of my friends. Dot was radiant, rejoicing, girlish in the halo of light from my torch. The steps had been no problem for her. The wind seemed to whip even more life and strength into her.

Next to Dot, Dick Craven stared out into the dark, his teeth clenched against the wet and wildness. Tragedy, decision, the beginnings of something new – that's what I thought I saw in his face.

Hartley was weeping unashamedly. All the way up the steps he had positioned himself behind Dot, ready to help if anything had gone wrong. Near the top I had heard him say excitedly, 'He *has* done it, Dot!' Now, he could only think about losing Nunc, and it made him cry.

I don't know how I looked. I felt wonderful. Someone had been healed when I prayed for her. I must be usable! I could have shouted my exhilaration over the parapet of the tower, waking the whole town to the fact that God *does* things.

In the middle of us, sheltered from the worst effects of the storm by our bodies, Nunc stood, only the very faintest of faint lights emanating from his body. When he spoke his voice was as clear and incisive as ever.

'Goodbye, David.'

'Thank you for being here, Nunc.'

'Goodbye, Dot. Thank you for comforting me.'

'Dear Nunc.'

'Goodbye, Richard.'

'Goodbye, Nunc – thanks.'

'Goodbye, Hartley, look after your church.'

'Bye,' choked Hartley, 'bye, Nunc . . .'

'Will you all cuddle me at the same time, please,' asked Nunc. Obediently we all moved inwards, intent on putting our arms round him, but as we met in the centre, we suddenly realized that he had gone, and instead of embracing an alien, we were embracing each other.

Postscript

Postscript

A fortnight before Nunc left, he and I spent an hour together one evening, just relaxing. He listened mostly, and I talked utter rubbish about all sorts of things, including the prayer book. I told him about Mr and Mrs Gesima, and their four daughters, Septua, Sexa, Quinqua and Quadra. He asked me what was meant by 'a table of movable feasts', and I said it was another name for a buffet supper, but he didn't know what I was talking about so I wished I hadn't bothered. Oh, and I told him about the time when Nick and Sue Clean-neck raised their arms at the family service, and little Adam Thornton said very loudly, 'Why are those two people surrendering to the Vicar, Mum?'

After rabbiting on like this for nearly an hour, I reached a sort of natural pause, and Nunc, doing one of his famous and disconcerting child-mystic switches, said, 'What is it you want to ask me, David?'

I believe one or more of my fellow scribes mentioned that I have red hair. That is true. It is also true that on those occasions when I blush I look like a hyper-active, mutant lobster. I must have looked like that when I answered Nunc's question.

'You've never told us who you are or where you come from,' I blurted out. 'It doesn't matter if you can't – or won't – I just thought you might give me a hint, or a clue, or . . . something,' I finished feebly.

Nunc stared at me with those big, luminous eyes of his for what must have been almost a minute, then his head dropped to one side and he wrinkled his nose reflectively.

'When one of my brothers was among you – only four or five years ago – ' he added, seeing the surprised look on my face, 'someone wrote something about him. He looked quite unlike myself because his task was quite different, and I am not authorized to say that the things this person wrote are correct, but they may offer a hint – or a clue.'

'But how can you – ?'

Nunc raised an arresting hand.

'I promise that on the morning after I leave you will find a copy of that writing, but I may not discuss it further on this day.'

On the morning following Nunc's departure I wandered over to the church, feeling a little bleak and Nuncless. It was cold and still inside, with just a ripple of something warm and wonderful passing through the air. I was about to leave when I noticed a sheet of paper lying on the top step in front of the altar. Sitting down on the step I scanned the neat handwriting that covered the sheet and realized, as I read, that Nunc had kept his promise.

Six o'clock, the sky that evening
Autumn grey, a shining dome.
The sun a glowing tangerine
That rolled along the far horizon
Don't remember where I'd been
He was just a shabby figure standing by the roadside
    near my home.
I parked the car and stood a while, enjoyed the way
    October daylight sweetly, sadly dies.

Then turned and walked towards the stranger
Don't know why
Except that when I passed I'd seen a warm and strange
    expression in his eyes
When I asked where he was heading he just smiled and
    said 'Well, now, my friend,
I don't believe I know,
But that's no reason not to go, unless you need me.'
'Come, eat with me,' I said 'and stay a while,
There's food for two, the sofa makes a fair to average
    bed.'
He said, 'Okay,' we went inside, I lit the lamps and
    poured some wine
We talked, and soon some orphan hope broke down the
    wall
And wept through every stumbling word of mine.

How the darkness circled round us
Like a disappointed foe.
It crouched and waited hungrily,
It filled the space behind the lamplight,
We were safe inside the glow.
And the wine was more than nectar, blood-red in the
    gleaming of the fire
His touch upon the bread disturbed me, something far
    beyond recall, or underground,
And then a smiling benediction
Seemed to fall
And work a little miracle, a relaxation in my heart. I
    heard a sound
My own voice, live with wakened passion, breaking
    with a nameless yearning

Like a long-forsaken child
Who is sick of running wild in desert places.
'Where's your home?' I asked, 'perhaps one day
I'll visit you.' His eyes were burning coals, he
whispered, 'Yes, I hope you will.'
We said goodnight, he slept, I wandered out, the air was
cold and clean
And looking up, for one eternal moment
I felt homesick for a place I'd never seen.

Later, when the day was breaking,
Later, when the day was there,
When I awoke in strange distress
To find the morning grey and silver
I was quick to rise and dress
Almost ran towards the stairway, hoping that my friend
would still be there.
But far away and in my mind, I seemed to hear a restless
ocean sighing to the shore
A sound like giant wings in motion.
Down below
The sheets and rugs were piled neatly, too much money
lay beside the door.
Though I called out through the doorway, in my heart I
knew he must be gone
The silence was profound
And the countryside around was cold and empty.
'Just one more day,' I said, 'he could have stayed.
To leave so soon with countless questions waiting to be
asked.'
I closed the door; inside, the fire was dead, but in the
silent air

A gentle warmth caressed the autumn morning
As it glowed and loved and softly lingered there.

And the words he spoke that evening
Were so full of love and light,
That the agony inside me
Was attacked and put to flight.
And you may believe I'm crazy
And I may believe you're right,
But I think it was an angel
I entertained that night.